Target: 20 Years of Design for All

Rizzoli
New York

New York · Paris · London · Milan

Futurists 14

Michael Graves 16

Philippe Starck 26

Hunter 36

FEED 42

Deborah Adler 48

TOMS 54

Tord Boontje 60

Dwell Magazine 62

Maximalists 68

Missoni 70

Liberty London 84

Lilly Pulitzer 96

Marimekko 116

Peter Pilotto 130

Thakoon 138

Prabal Gurung 144

Optimists 152

Todd Oldham 154

Sonia Kashuk 160

Cynthia Rowley 162

Marcus Samuelsson 168

Isabel and Ruben Toledo 170

Museum of Ice Cream 172

Askov Finlayson 176

John Derian 178

Oh Joy! 182

Harajuku Mini 184

Chris March 190

Luella Bartley 192

Romantics
196

Isaac Mizrahi
198

Jason Wu
212

Victoria Beckham
220

Altuzarra
230

Proenza Schouler
238

Kate Young
244

Neiman Marcus
250

Phillip Lim
256

Zac Posen
266

Jonathan Saunders
272

Erin Fetherston
276

Mavericks
280

Alexander McQueen
282

Anna Sui
292

Fiorucci
300

Jean Paul Gaultier
308

Stephen Burrows
316

Rodarte
322

Stephen Sprouse
328

Introduction
6

Foreword
8

Afterword
344

Index
348

Credits
350

Acknowledgments
351

Dreaming and Doing

Introduction by Todd Waterbury,
Chief Creative Officer, Target

My first reaction to the audacity of Charles and Ray Eames' quote on design was immediate and conflicting. It pushed away everything I believed, while pulling me closer. How could what they said be true, and how was it possible? As I began studying the work of these American design pioneers, it became clear this quote wasn't a statement of their process or their ideology, it was a startling kind of California dreaming: "We want to make the best for the most for the least."

But it doesn't work that way.

We've all been taught the basic laws of balance, of economics. In order to gain something of value, to increase availability, or achieve some form of greater enjoyment, something else must give. It's the zero-sum game of compromising and cutting. You. Can't. Have. It. All.

We're fortunate, though, that there are others among us who don't settle as comfortably into those neatly drawn lines of rational, binary thought. Instead, they are restless, fueled by possibility and progress. They know that design is the bridge between dreaming it and doing it.

Design has been central to the DNA of the Target brand for decades. We see design as more than a process—it's a path. Where others see obstacles in the tension between competing visions or conflicting goals, we see the space to go somewhere new and create something better. That's why a this-can't-be-possible tension lives at the center of our brand promise, "Expect More. Pay Less."

Nowhere has the meaning of that promise been seen as universally—and felt as personally—than through our creation of the design collaboration in 1999. The concept was at once a celebration and a radical declaration, delivered in three words: "Design for All."

To proclaim that design, which for so many of us then, was defined by its virtue and desirability, prized precisely because it wasn't for everyone, should now be for everyone was revolutionary. That idea just didn't exist. Design was appreciated only by those who understood its creative and cultural codes. Design was experienced by, and available to, those who could afford the version that looked better, worked better, felt better. Having design in your life was having joy in your life. So, the question (and the tension) was how could this joy—created for the few—be made available to all?

How could we make the best for the most for the least?

The first answer didn't appear on our shelves, but in public. It was our first design collaboration, made with the architect Michael Graves, a luminous, futuristic "blueprint" sheath designed to encase the Washington Monument during its renovation. It was a 555-foot statement of intent: that Target believed design's role in society was to enhance everyone's every day. That generous gesture inspired the 150-piece Michael Graves for Target collection that followed. It was the first time so many beautiful-, playful-, and well-designed objects for living were affordable to so many.

What began as a radical declaration—"Design for All"—has become a symbol of progress for Target and culture at large. It not only inspired the next 174 Target collaborations over the next 20 years, with many of the most celebrated and influential designers of our time, but changed the definition of design altogether. It erased those neatly drawn lines of rational, binary thought. It enabled us the clarity, conviction and courage to pursue a noble dream: that putting more joy within reach is what lifts us all up.

Opposite: Charles and Ray Eames, photographed by Arnold Newman

Hey Hey, Tar-jay

Foreword by Kim Hastreiter, an editor, curator, and cultural anthropologist who co-founded *PAPER* magazine

To me, Target isn't just a store but an old friend.

It was eons ago that I saw my very first Target store. I was still a teenager and slightly traumatized on that late summer day in 1969. I'd just hopped a plane with my mom and dad. I was leaving my childhood home in New Jersey, headed to St. Louis, Missouri, to enroll in my first year of college at Washington University. I'd never been to the Midwest before and still remember the stomachache and my disorientation the day I moved into my dorm room. That same day, my parents schlepped me to my first Target, a new go-to "discount" store not far from campus.

Growing up in a New Jersey town right outside New York City, we had never heard of Target. But St. Louis locals knew it well, as the brand—the brainchild of the famed Minneapolis department store team Dayton and Hudson—had just launched their exciting family-friendly discount concept in the Midwest. This particular outlet was a celebrated newcomer to St. Louis. The fluorescent-lit variety store was in a nearby mini-mall and served as the spot for inexpensive dorm necessities like cleaning supplies, laundry baskets, toothpaste, light bulbs, brooms, and garbage cans. We *oohed* and *aahed* over the low prices, stocked up like crazy, and settled me into my room.

Once school began, it didn't take long for me to see that liberal arts studies and dorm life wasn't really for me. By the middle of that first year, I had not only decided to drop my normal classes and enroll in the university's art school, but I had transformed from a wholesome, preppy New Jersey girl into a counterculture hippie, moving off campus to a dumpy apartment. I ditched my skirt and cardigan sets for long, flowing Indian dresses accessorized with hiking boots, Moroccan beads, and fringed vests. My parents were now the ones traumatized when they flew in to visit me. I know they were totally shocked—and likely horrified—to see the new me, but as open-minded East Coasters and amazingly wise and encouraging parents, they bit their tongues and supported me, gently guiding me to the local Target store once again for a big shopping spree, where I imagine they hoped to clean me and my apartment up a bit. I might have been anti-establishment at that moment, but I was secretly grateful to have my folks bring me to the aisles of Target so they could help organize my hippie pad—not to mention buy me a treasure trove of art supplies in support of my new goal of becoming an artist.

After a few years, I left the Midwest and the land of Target to follow my art dreams, driving to Canada where I began wearing only black and studying conceptual art with legends like Joseph Beuys and Vito Acconci at Nova Scotia College of Art and Design. After graduation, I headed to Los Angeles for graduate school where I continued my studies for a few more years with my new mentor, artist John Baldessari, at California Institute of the Arts. It was still the 70s and sadly the first Target didn't open in California until 1983, so I was a bit lost when settling into my Santa Monica digs. California cheered up my serious, all-black, conceptual life, and by the time I got my masters degree I was accessorizing my black clothes with leopard tube tops and gold leather Springolators. By now I was well prepared for my ambitious return to hit New York City hard and make my mark. NYC was a mecca in those days for a creative person. An extraordinary collaborative community of talent was exploding downtown below 14th Street—filmmakers were working with artists, artists with musicians, and fashion designers with artists and musicians. I eagerly jumped in. To pay the rent while figuring out how to make a career for myself, I sold clothes in a fancy but eccentric Madison

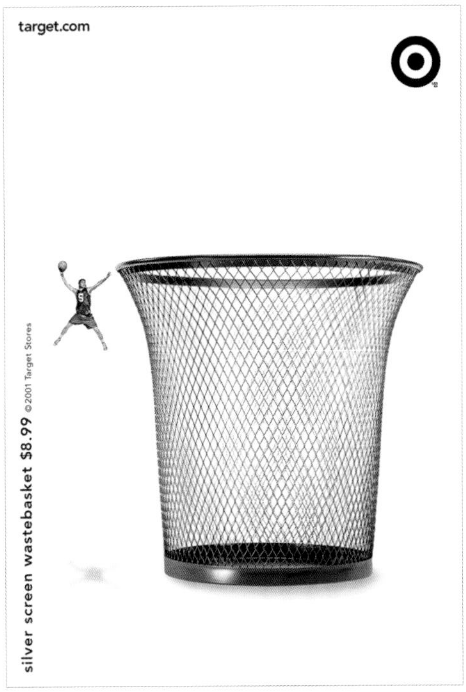

target.com
silver screen wastebasket $8.99 ©2001 Target Stores

Opposite:
Portrait of Kim by Maira Kalman

New York Times newspaper advertisements, spotted by Kim Hastreiter

Avenue shop where I fell in love with fashion and befriended *New York Times* photographer Bill Cunningham, who photographed me on the street every day coming out of the subway in my crazy outfits. He berated me daily for working as a shopgirl when he knew I was an artist. Eventually he got me a job as the style editor of a supercool, respected downtown weekly—even though I had zero experience.

This new job changed my life. I loved bringing my friends—who were artists, designers, musicians, and photographers—together on my pages every week. Collaboration became my mantra. I worked with artists like Robert Mapplethorpe to photograph fashion, Kenny Scharf to illustrate my home-design supplement, and Keith Haring—who modeled for my crazy Halloween shoot dressed like Frankenstein's monster. The designer Vivienne Westwood asked me to introduce her to my friend Keith, who was not yet famous. She wanted to collaborate with him on her next collection. In those days, Westwood and her music impresario husband, Malcolm McLaren, were my heroes. Every season, Malcolm would make an album and Vivienne would do a fashion collection to go with it. I convinced Keith to do it although he had no idea who Westwood was. The results were amazing and are now in museums around the world and in my dresser drawers, as we were all paid in clothing instead of money! Looking back, I think this was the seminal moment that I got bitten by what I call the "collaboration bug." It also helps me understand where my future obsession with Target came from decades later, when they'd begin to create incredible and historical collaborations with artists and designers.

Then one day, our weekly paper suddenly folded and my job disappeared. It was a huge shock because I'd fallen in love with the democratic idea of using media instead of traditional galleries to show art and distribute ideas to the world. I didn't want a normal job, so some friends and I started a monthly zine at my kitchen table with a few thousand dollars called *PAPER*. Here, our creative community could have a voice and we could shine light on the talented people coming up at that important cultural moment in New York City. The year was 1984.

Our new little baby, *PAPER*, was a big scrappy hit. Each issue was like a party. Time passed, and we eked by and kept growing—even though we were as poor as church mice. We survived on advertising revenue, but it was difficult. Our circulation was small and our content edgy, which wasn't appealing to ad agencies more concerned with quantity than quality of readers. We'd feature unknowns on the cover who would always become hot a few years later, which was bad for business but got us attention. *PAPER* became the place where folks would look to find the next big thing. We began getting requests from brands that wanted to connect with our influential, early-adopter community, so we started a little agency to help pay our bills.

One day in 2001, I noticed an amazing little black-and-white fractional ad in the front section of my morning *New York Times*. It showed a miniature man shooting a basketball into a gigantic metal mesh garbage can (costing $8.99). Looking closer, I saw that it was an ad for Target! When I flipped the page I saw another ad with a tiny little man sticking his tongue out to lick an enormous ice cream scooper ($7.99). Then a third, showing a miniature couple shaking coconuts from a gigantic feather duster ($5.99) resembling a palm tree! OMG—I was stunned!

The idea that a low-priced, mass-market convenience store would advertise in such a high-end environment, next to posh luxury ads like Tiffany's and Chanel, blew my mind. Every day, I rushed to open my *Times* to see what the next little black-and-white Target ads would be. They always amazed me, and I became totally obsessed with finding out what as going on at this big Midwestern discount store. As a collaboration freak, I went even more nuts when I discovered many of the inexpensive products in these ads—from toasters to teakettles to ice cream scoopers were from a kitchen collection they'd done with the famous architect Michael Graves. This sparked my intense curiosity. It was completely unheard of and radical to have a low-priced mass retailer work with a high-end designer to create beautiful products that were affordable for all. This really struck a nerve with me as I'd always been troubled by the question of why great style or great design had to be expensive. A good idea isn't more expensive than a bad idea, so good design shouldn't cost more than bad design. I never believed money was always necessary to create great work. After all, we had been making a great magazine on a shoestring for more than a decade. Our lack of resources only enhanced our ingenuity and forced us to be more innovative than magazines with lots of money.

Target had expanded quite a bit since I'd shopped there in my college days. The more I sniffed around, the more excited I became. I soon found out from a designer friend of mine, Todd Oldham, that Target had contacted him to design a collection. Then, a few weeks later, another good friend of mine, the designer and artist Stephen Sprouse, called to tell me Target had contacted him to do a collection as well! *WOW*. I smelled a scoop. I was exhilarated by this groundbreaking idea of making great design accessible and decided to do a big feature on Target for my next design issue. I began calling Target headquarters daily to try to interview someone about what was going on. Who was doing these ads? What was up with all these collaborations with my friends? Trouble was that Target, in those days, had an old-school secrecy policy, so they wouldn't talk. I'd saved a big bank of pages for this story that I now had to fill. Frustrated, I decided I just had to make up my own feature. If Target wouldn't talk to me, I'd just invite all my designer and artist friends to design an everyday object under $15 for TAR-JAY (as folks had begun calling it) and run it in *PAPER!* Everyone I asked loved the idea and agreed enthusiastically, sending me amazing designs. Manolo Blahnik did a shoehorn, Kate Spade designed gardening tools, Pierre Cardin did a plastic coffeepot, Isaac Mizrahi drew moth "cubes" (instead of balls, so they wouldn't roll all over), Geoffrey Beene designed garbage bags, Vladimir Kagan did a toilet brush, and Ingo Maurer designed a flashlight attachment to transform it into a mood lamp. I then snuck my friend, the legendary design guru Murray Moss, into the new Target store just opened in Queens, and surreptitiously interviewed him about their radical display of everyday merchandise. We both agreed that the interior of the Target stores had been reimagined in a very pop-art aesthetic that Andy Warhol would have loved. In the end, my editorial was epic and ran on 26 pages in *PAPER's* April 2002 design issue. It was one of my favorite pieces I've ever done in my 33-year career at *PAPER*. And guess what? The Target powers that be crept out of hiding—calling me the day of release to tell me they loved it and invited me to meet them for lunch the following week. Within a month I began working with Target (via *PAPER*), and I've been whispering in their ear ever since. For the past 17 years, I have witnessed

every single one of their extraordinary collaborations (over 150!), working on and shopping like crazy at many of them.

I'll never forget the night in 2002 when I climbed aboard a Target boat that had just sailed down the Hudson (docking at a West Side pier in NYC) to shop Todd Oldham's collection. I think this was the first pop-up store in history! Or when I brought my friend the designer Duro Olowu to the 2006 Target launch party of designer Behnaz Sarafpour's collection atop Rockefeller Center—with the secret motive to pitch Duro for a Target collab. The collab never materialized, but that night I did introduce Duro to my friend Thelma Golden, the director of the Studio Museum in Harlem, who eventually became his wife. There were so many other epic moments. The amazing Vertical Fashion Show that Target put on in Midtown, where acrobat/models scaled the side of an office building, reimagining the skyscraper as a runway. Or the bedlam at the huge Missoni for Target launch, where racks were stripped bare in minutes by armies of hysterical fashionistas. Or the time when Isaac Mizrahi held a huge runway show mixing his couture with his Target collection at Fashion Week, showing $3000 skirts with $29 Mizrahi for Target sweater designs. It was a seminal and brilliant high-low moment.

I've amassed incredible items from Target's collaborations over the years—including my late friend Stephen Sprouse's blow-up lounge chair. Stephen would phone me in the middle of the night from where he was holed up in Minneapolis, working on his collection. One Target exec had to take meetings with him after dinner as he'd sleep all day and work all night. She was a good sport about it and would often bring her kids to the meetings—Stephen would always try to charm and pitch his more outrageous designs to them so their mom would say yes. I remember he once pitched the children a skimpy men's Speedo-style bathing suit and webbed-feet scuba socks. They were both rejected by mom as unsellable, even though her kids loved them. Then there's my favorite apron and oven mitts that I got my chef-friend Marcus Samuelsson to design a decade ago for the Harlem Target store opening. We did it all on my office computer at *PAPER*, using colorful drawings of fruits and veggies he had the neighborhood kids make. My closets are stuffed with bath towels by artists like Kehinde Wiley and Jeff Koons from when I connected Target to the Art Production Fund to produce and sell them at Art Basel. I still eat breakfast on my gorgeous 2003 Isaac Mizrahi flower dishes and sip from my paisley Lilly Pulitzer coffee cups on my colorful Marimekko place mats. Everywhere I look in my home, I see Target collabs—my Missoni computer case, my Peter Pilotto tote bag, my iconic Stephen Burrows jersey T-shirt, my Isabel Toledo sarongs, and so much more.

I guess you can tell by now that, to me, Target isn't just a store but an old friend. That's why I was so grateful to be invited to write the foreword for this wonderful book celebrating two decades of groundbreaking collaborations with this unique and trailblazing American brand that I adore. So, thank you, Target, and cheers to continuing your magic and collaborative spirit. We all can't wait to see the surprise and delight your next 20 years will bring! Bravo!

Excerpts from *PAPER* magazine's April 2002 design issue, where Kim Hastreiter asked famous designers to create their dream Target products.

RUBEN AND ISABEL TOLEDO

Sale Sale Sale 4.99 per pair

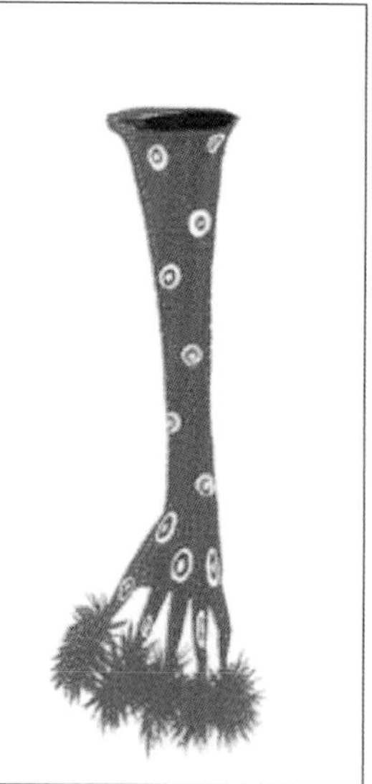

Rubber toilet scrub-gloves (with sponge fingers)

TOLAND GRINNELL

Domestic-wipe caddy

EXPECT MORE PAY LESS 19.00

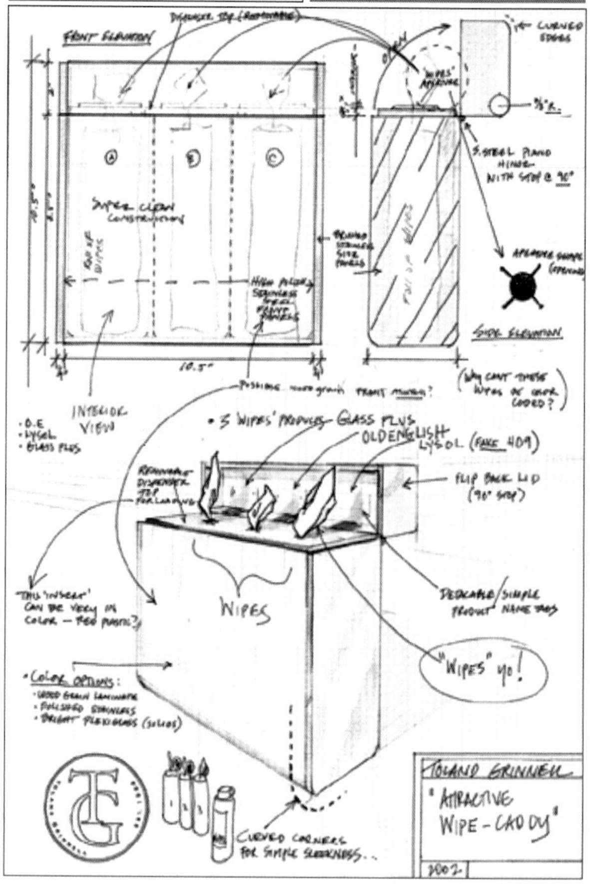

MANOLO BLAHNIK

Shoehorn shaped like a high-heel. Made of solid aluminum.

EXPECT MORE PAY LESS 7.98

EXTRA ORDINARY DESIGN

INGO MAURER

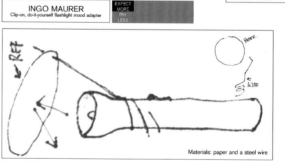

Clip-on, do-it-yourself flashlight mood adapter

EXPECT MORE PAY LESS

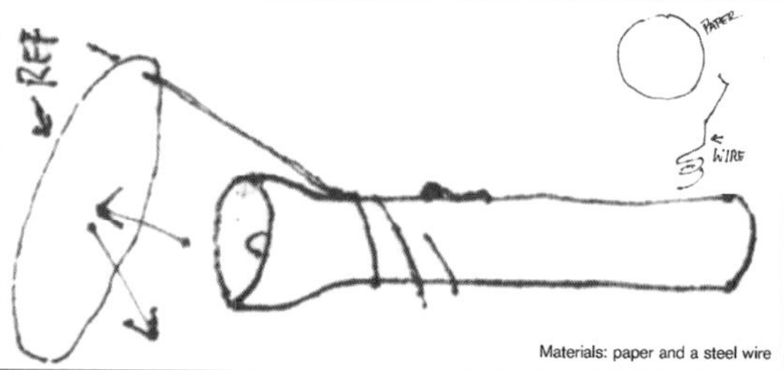

Materials: paper and a steel wire

Maurer: "The world does not need one more flashlight. My adapter-reflector turns an ordinary flashlight into a mood light. Use it on a dinner table. It's more pleasant than a candle."

TUCKER VIEMEISTER

Astroturf flip-flop

EXPECT MORE PAY LESS 12.99

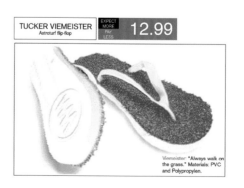

Viemeister: "Always walk on the grass." Materials: PVC and Polypropylen.

Sale Sale Sale 5.99

GEOFFREY BEENE
His and hers garbage bags

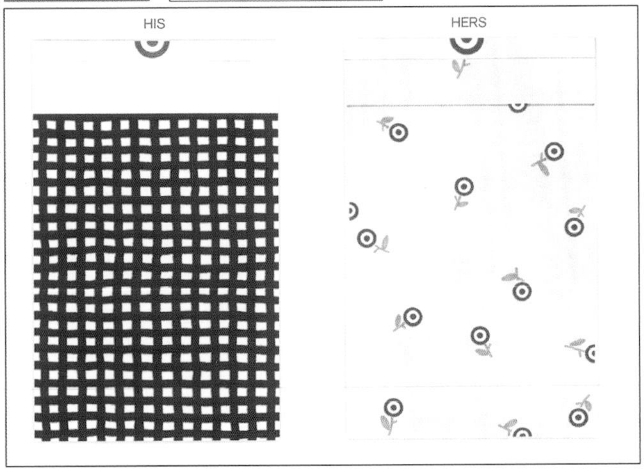

Sale Sale Sale 6.99
for 36 bags

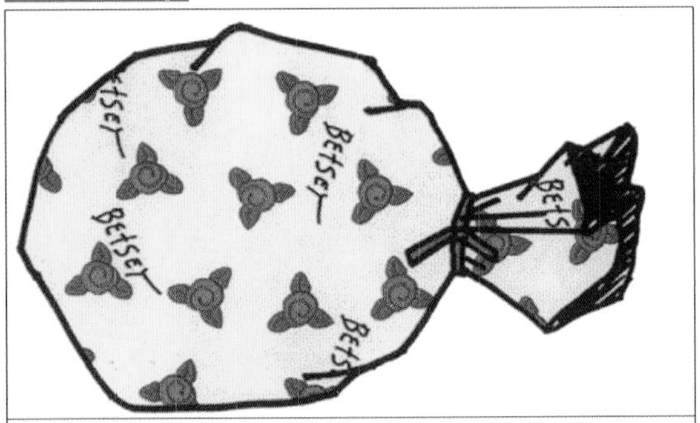

BETSEY JOHNSON
Lawn and leaf bags

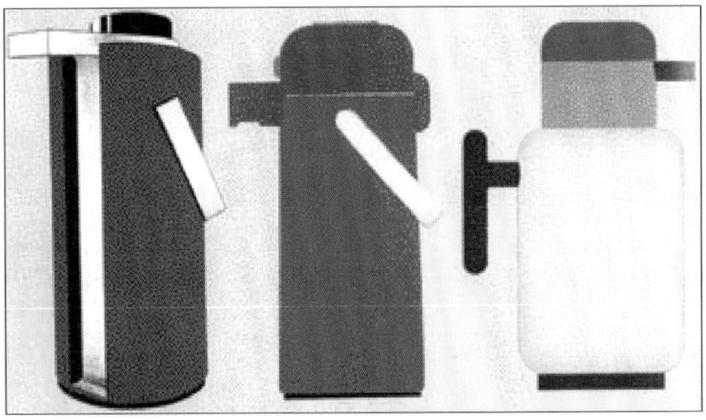

PIERRE CARDIN
Coffee pots and thermos

EXPECT MORE PAY LESS 12.99
to 14.99

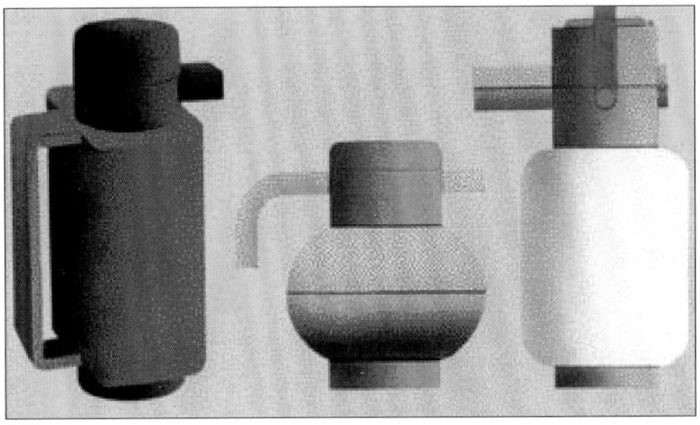

"Toilet brushes that need not be hidden."

VLADIMIR KAGAN Toilet brushes

Sale Sale Sale 5.99

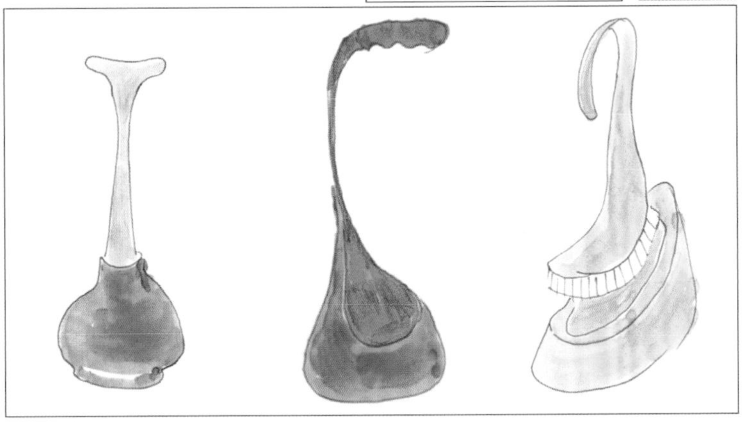

Watering tin — Sale Sale Sale 4.69

KATE SPADE

Sale Sale Sale 11.69

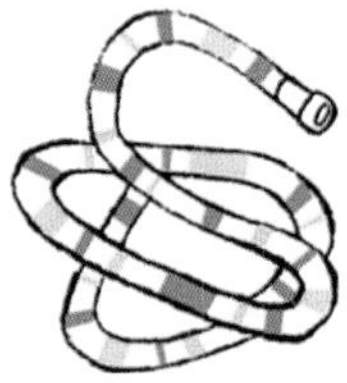

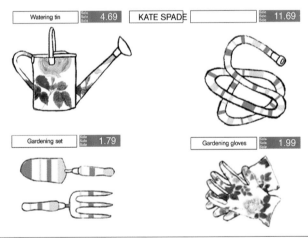

Gardening set — Sale Sale Sale 1.79

Gardening gloves — Sale Sale Sale 1.99

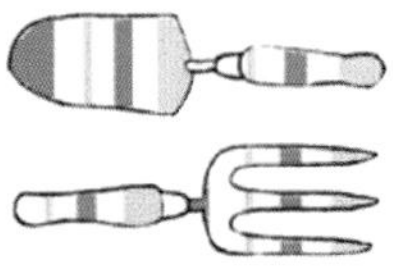

Sagmeister: "The stool is always clean—you just tear off a new sheet. It could be made with different paper, so that it can change its mood and color."

Mizrahi: "Moth balls are a thing of the past. They roll around and are messy."

Sale Sale Sale 7.99

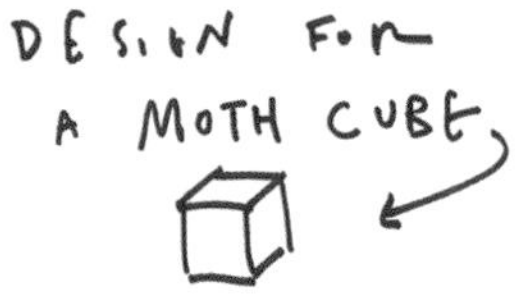

Actual size: about as big as a sugar cube
Scent: to be discussed

ISAAC MIZRAHI
The moth cube

Thermos — Sale Sale

ANDY SPADE FOR JACK SPADE

Plastic beer cooler — Sale Sale Sale 7.59

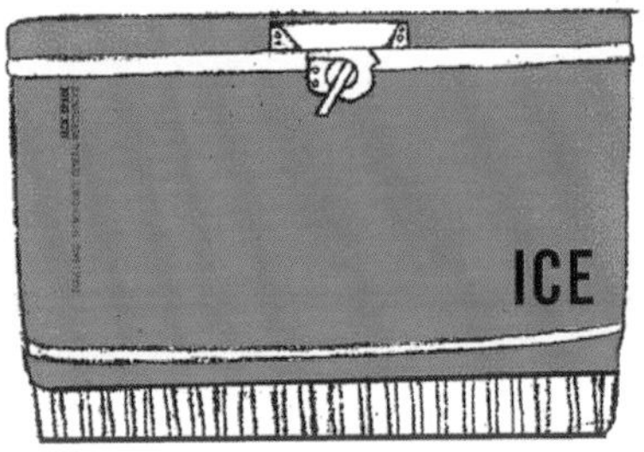

A sippy cup resembling a royal chalice? A pill bottle revolutionizing prescription medication in America? Futuristic design isn't all robots, voice-controlled appliances and airborne cars. Most of the time it's found in things we use every day—a kettle, a chair, a rubber boot—reimagined in ways that spark joy in their users. For these visionaries, be it Michael Graves or Hunter, design involves exploring the limits of what's known for what could be, using state-of-the-art technology and materials pushed to extremes.

Michael Graves
1999-2013

Philippe Starck
2002

Hunter
2018

FEED
2013

Deborah Adler
2005-2015

TOMS
2014

Tord Boontje
2006

Dwell Magazine
2016-2017

Futurists

Michael
Graves
1999-2013

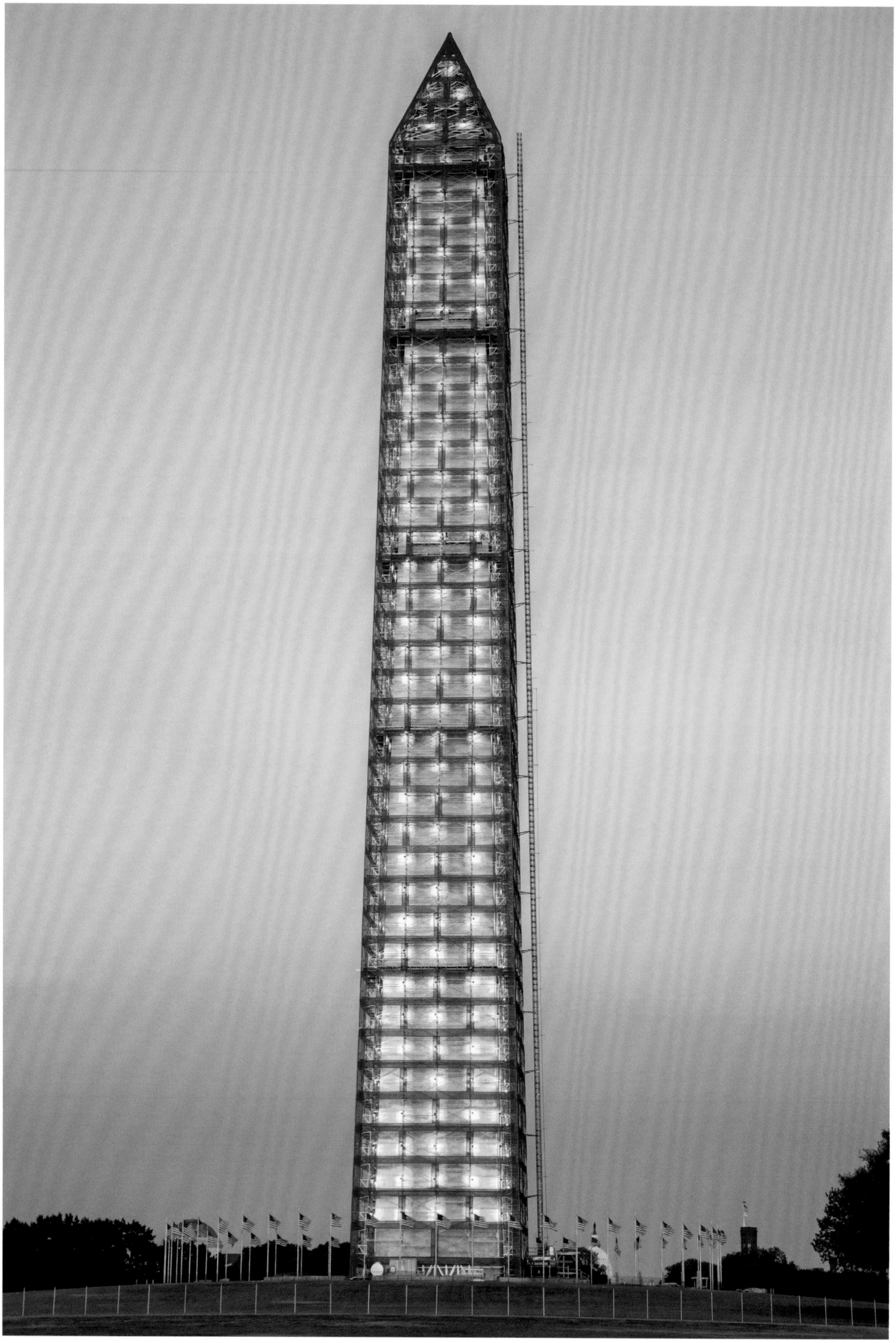

Wrapping Buildings and Radicalizing Objects with Michael Graves

Michael Graves, photographed by Chris Felver, 2000

Opposite: The Washington Monument covered in Michael Graves' scaffolding, photographed by Charles O. Cecil, 2013

Following spread: A set of custom playing cards sent to media, illustrating the 2003 Michael Graves for Target collection. The limited edition box features a white Target bullseye and reads "The Big Deal."

The Michael Graves partnership—our first with a major designer and architect—didn't start with products you could buy in our stores. It began with a building you could wrap: the 555-foot Washington Monument. In 1997, Target funded the structure's restoration, and, rather than hiding it under the cladding and padding of traditional scaffolding, we decided to enlist the American architect Michael Graves to come up with an innovative solution—one that wasn't a public eyesore.

He covered the obelisk in a grid of electric blue fabric, which mimicked—and exaggerated—the original pattern below. Like a high-tech crosshatch, it lit up every night, allowing the structure beneath to glow in its original glory—even during renovation. So popular was the redesigned scaffolding that other cities, from Minneapolis to Pittsburgh, wanted to recreate the project for themselves.

Like much of Graves' work, the scaffolding was for everyone: open-minded, open-hearted and (quite literally) open-faced. Later, the designer had lunch with our team and we asked him to reimagine household objects, making them a little more considered and user-friendly. So he did.

Over the course of our 15-year partnership, we released more than 2,000 objects. From teakettles to spatulas, candlesticks to faucet handles, our cheerful, modernist creations with Graves touched every corner of the home. It was the first time he had ever sold a consumer range of products: we wrapped them up simply in calm blue, like a blueprint. As critic Paul Goldberger wrote: "Thanks to mass merchandising, a tiny piece of an architect's oeuvre is within the reach of everyone."

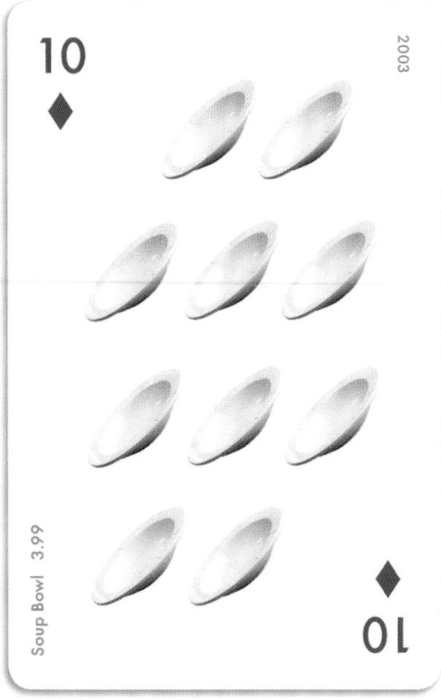
10
2003
Soup Bowl 3.99
10

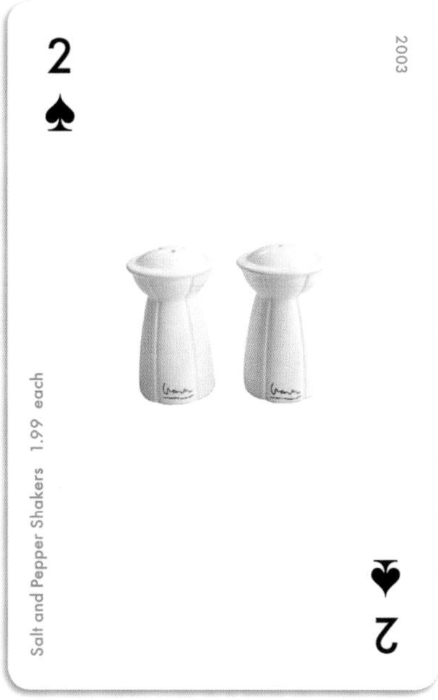
2
2003
Salt and Pepper Shakers 1.99 each
2

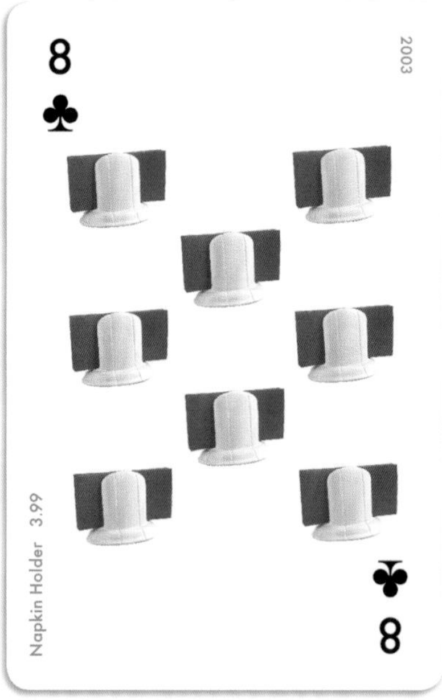
8
2003
Napkin Holder 3.99
8

9
Wood Feather Duster 7.99

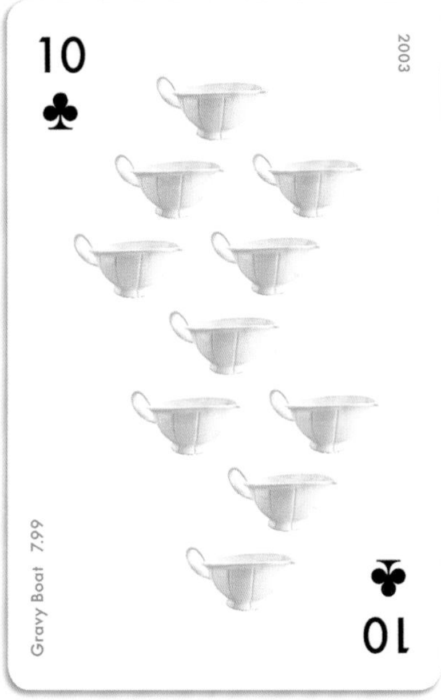
10
2003
Gravy Boat 7.99
10

2
2003
Jellyroll Pan 14.99
2

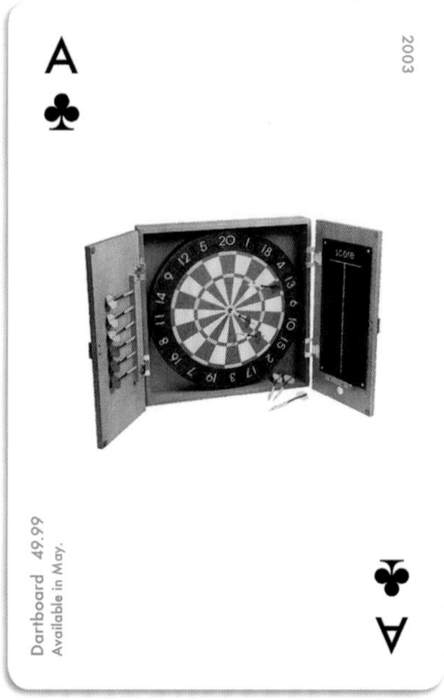
A
2003
Dartboard 49.99
Available in May.
A

4
Clock Radio 19.99

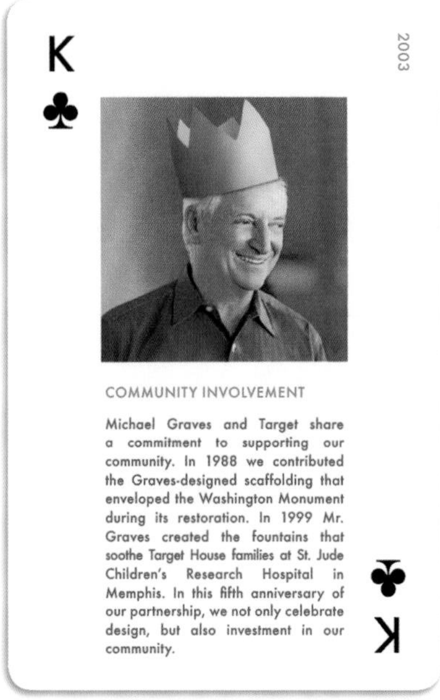
K
2003
COMMUNITY INVOLVEMENT
Michael Graves and Target share a commitment to supporting our community. In 1988 we contributed the Graves-designed scaffolding that enveloped the Washington Monument during its restoration. In 1999 Mr. Graves created the fountains that soothe Target House families at St. Jude Children's Research Hospital in Memphis. In this fifth anniversary of our partnership, we not only celebrate design, but also investment in our community.
K

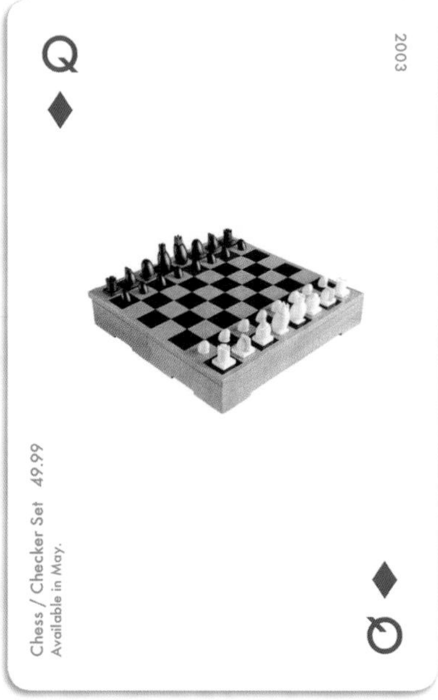
Q
2003
Chess / Checker Set 49.99
Available in May.
Q

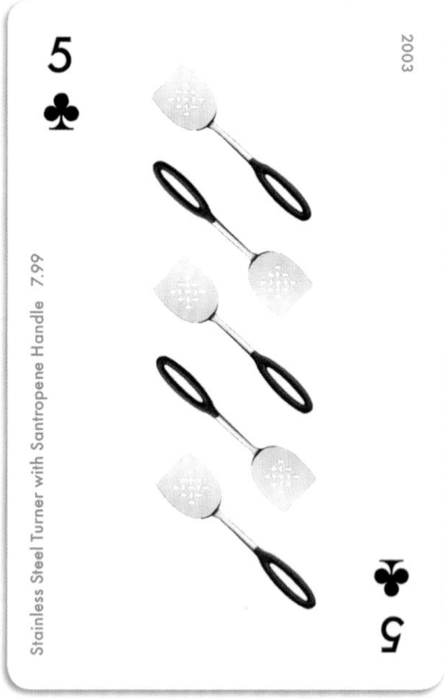
5
2003
Stainless Steel Turner with Santropene Handle 7.99
5

4
Digital Scale 49.99

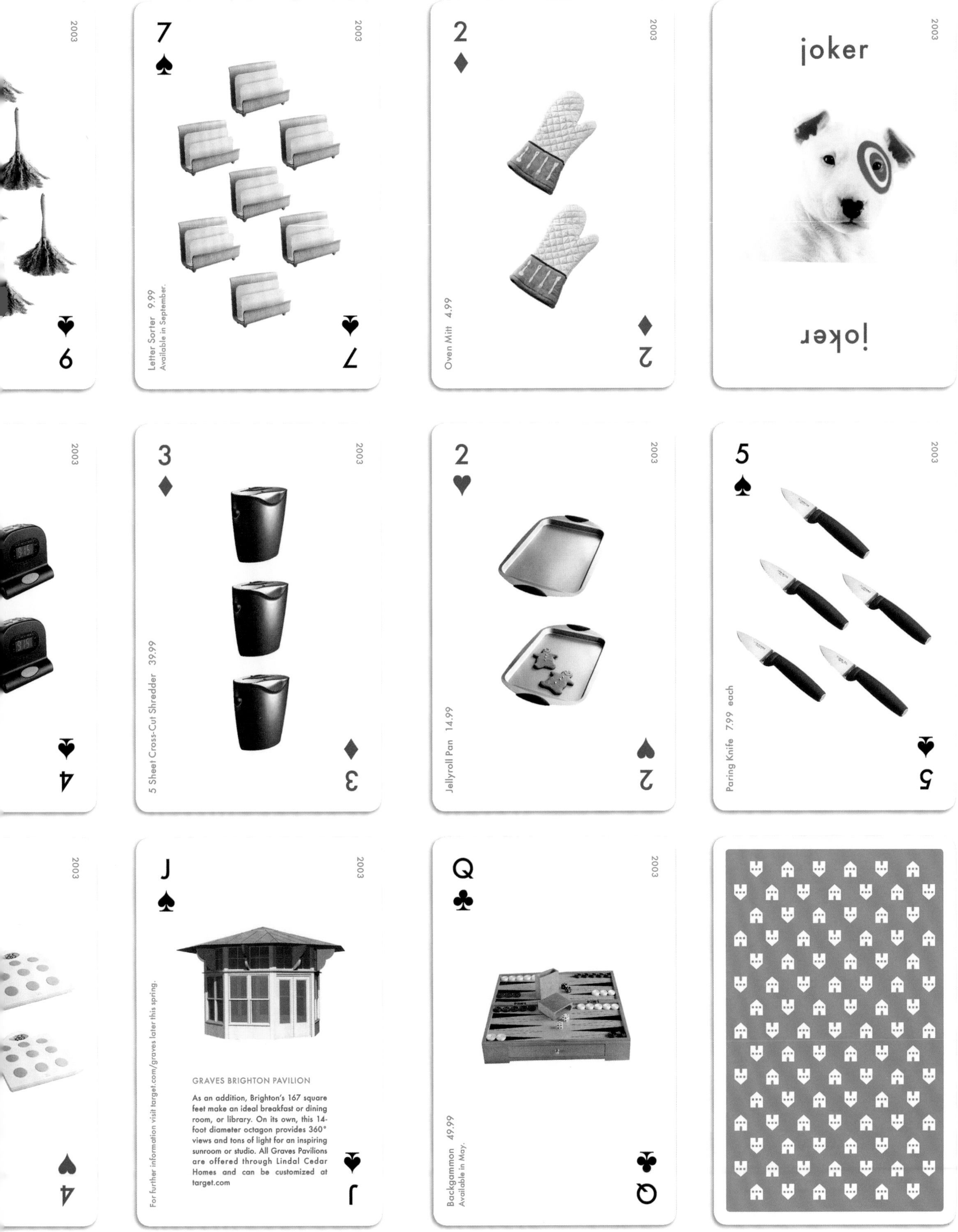
2003
9
7
Letter Sorter 9.99
Available in September.
2
Oven Mitt 4.99
joker
joker
4
3
5 Sheet Cross-Cut Shredder 39.99
2
Jellyroll Pan 14.99
5
Paring Knife 7.99 each
4
J
For further information visit target.com/graves later this spring.
GRAVES BRIGHTON PAVILION
As an addition, Brighton's 167 square feet make an ideal breakfast or dining room, or library. On its own, this 14-foot diameter octagon provides 360° views and tons of light for an inspiring sunroom or studio. All Graves Pavilions are offered through Lindal Cedar Homes and can be customized at target.com
Q
Backgammon 49.99
Available in May.

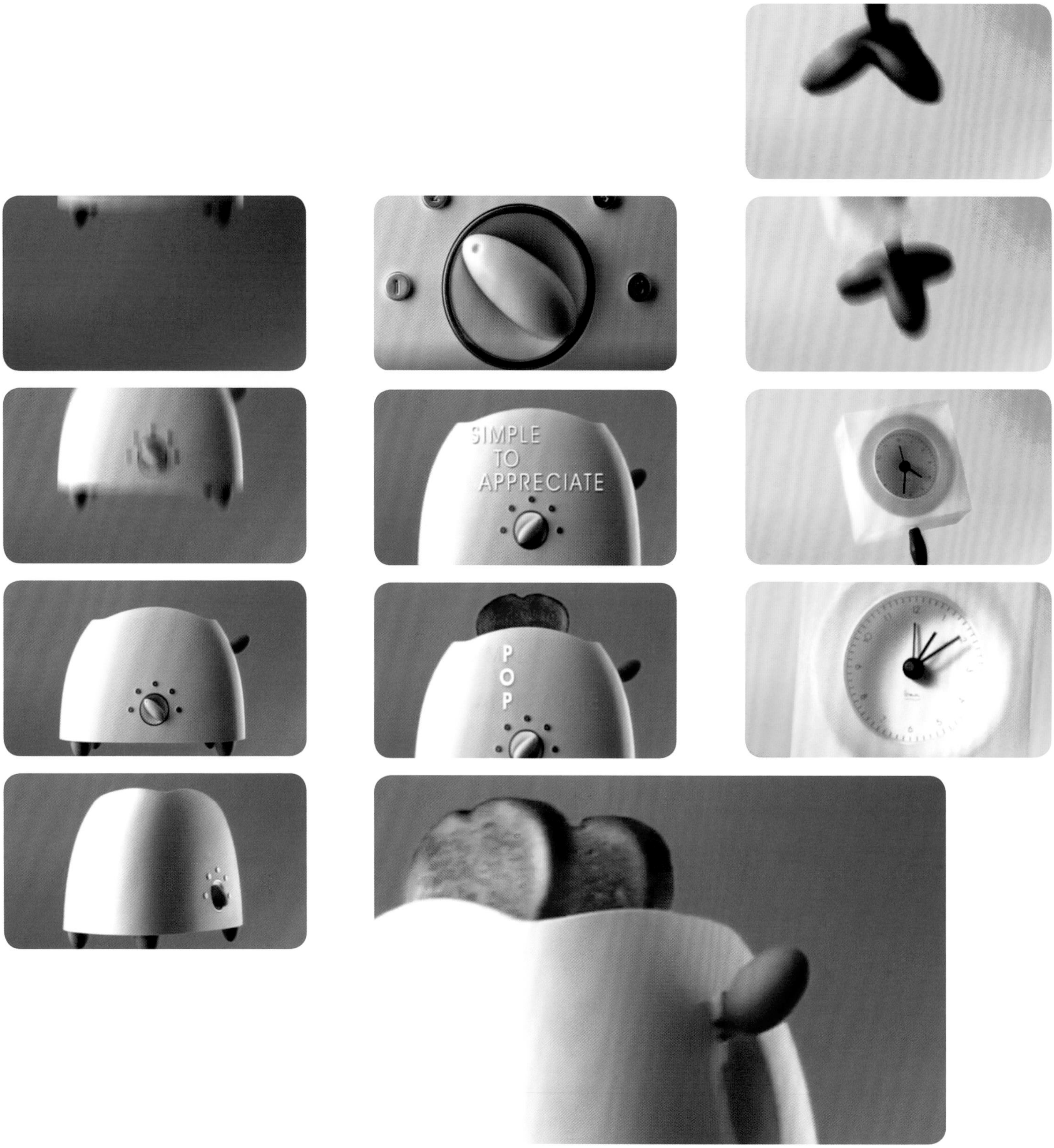

Stills from the
Michael Graves for
Target TV commercial

Opposite:
Telephone from
the Michael Graves
for Target collection

It's not just the form and shape of Graves' objects that I love. It's his touch of whimsy that gives them life, emotion, and heart.

Patrick Douglas, Director of Strategy and Advanced Development, Product Design and Development at Target

To me, great design isn't a beautiful rug with perfectly placed pillows. It's the way a well-designed teakettle reminds you to have a cup and slow down.

In Conversation with Michael Graves Superfan Bobby Berk

Interview by Robin Ekiss

Growing up in small-town Missouri, Bobby Berk dreamed of moving to the big city. With just a few bucks in his pocket and no job prospects in sight, he made his move to New York in 2003, working his way up the retail ranks to head his own design brand. As resident design guru on Netflix's *Queer Eye*, Berk's name has become synonymous with stylish interiors, but he's never forgotten where he came from or his first experience with affordable design, our where-it-all-started collection with Michael Graves.

ROBIN EKISS So, let me take you back. You walk into Target as a kid, and see Michael Graves' products on shelves. What was that like?
BOBBY BERK It was a really important moment for me—the first time I realized design could make people happy! Anyone can fall in love with a piece of art that speaks to them, but seeing an entire collection that was practical? That felt like magic.

RE So many of those Graves designs have become iconic, like the teakettle, the toaster, and the telephone. Which pieces stood out the most for you, and why?
BB This might sound surprising, but his spatula made the biggest impact on me. The thought he put into something so simple, [something] you use every day. It was functional and pretty. And the kettle's shape stood out to me, too. It was unconventional, angular and so chic. Yes, a teakettle was chic! You wanted to stare at it; it wasn't an eyesore on the counter.

RE Sounds like you had an emotional connection to that design. Do you think we need to have that sense of connection in order to consider something great design?
BB Honestly, it's all subjective! If you love something, you're going to consider it great design. Maybe someone will disagree with you, but that's the beauty of design: it's all personal preference. The best piece of advice I can give (even though you didn't ask!) is to buy what you like. There's no right or wrong answer when it comes to your opinion.

RE Do you think seeing examples of considered design at such a young age set you on a path to a career in design?
BB I've always looked at things differently. I've always been inspired by the subtleties of things, like that spatula. Like anyone, my taste evolves and changes. I'm still on my journey, and it's fun being inspired by artists who spark creativity along the way.

RE Since we're talking about creativity, let's talk about your work on *Queer Eye*. Your designs—like Graves'—are both serious and playful. How does having access to great, affordable design make a difference in someone's life?
BB People always say that things don't make you happy, but at the end of the day, they do. Making great design affordable means anyone can have it. Historically, it's typically only for people with money, but Target brings these collaborations to the front line, so everyone can have designer items that make them happy.

RE So happiness doesn't have a price?
BB Things that make you happy don't need to be expensive. They just need to be something you're passionate about.

RE What are some of the most common design challenges you see when you're working with clients on *Queer Eye*?
BB The biggest challenge is functionality—not having your space organized to make life easier. So often, the way people's houses are set up actually makes their lives harder. When your day starts out with chaos, it ends in chaos. My challenge is figuring out how a home can best work for people, and arranging the décor and tools to make how they live feel smarter, not harder. An organized space is a happy space.

RE You call your clients on the show "heroes." Do you think seeing the world from others' perspectives (and helping them see yours) has made you a more empathetic designer?
BB I think I was chosen for *Queer Eye* because I'm an incredibly empathetic person. I try to put myself in the shoes of everyone I design for, and I take our heroes' journeys very personally. I'll never forget where I came from, and that it wasn't easy. I know how important and how hard it is to turn yourself around. Having a pretty place isn't the answer, but the pride of taking care of where you live can make you happier every day.

RE Would you say a well-designed space comes from a personal place, not just a professional one?
BB When I'm designing a space, I think about how to create connectivity with people. Design has a huge impact on our day-to-day lives. Whether it's with family or inviting guests into your home, setting up a kitchen that works for your household makes your day seamless. The same goes for living rooms. You should think, "How can I set up this space to best cultivate conversation?" instead of just facing everyone toward the TV. Home is where the heart is, right?

RE What other simple design touches can make a house feel more like a home?
BB I love plants! I put all my plants on rollers because they're heavy and when I want to be creative, I can move them around.

RE Do you think culture shapes design, or is it the other way around?
BB Culture definitely shapes design! Different parts of the world take different approaches to design. But with shows like *Queer Eye*, we're also showing people that design has a huge impact on your day-to-day. It may not change your life, but how your home functions and looks can have an effect on your happiness.

RE Have your feelings about design changed over time?
BB When I was younger I was surrounded by and inspired by design, but I didn't think it affected my life. As I've gotten older and want to spend more time at home, I've realized that how you set up your place can jump-start your day or help you end it calmly.

RE What does great design mean to you today?
BB To me, great design isn't a beautiful rug with perfectly placed pillows. It's being intentional about where you hang your coat after a long day. It's the way a well-designed teakettle reminds you to have a cup and slow down.

Bobby Berk, photographed by Silvia Razgova, 2018

Opposite: Spatula from the Michael Graves for Target collection

Philippe
Starck
2002

S+ARCK™ +

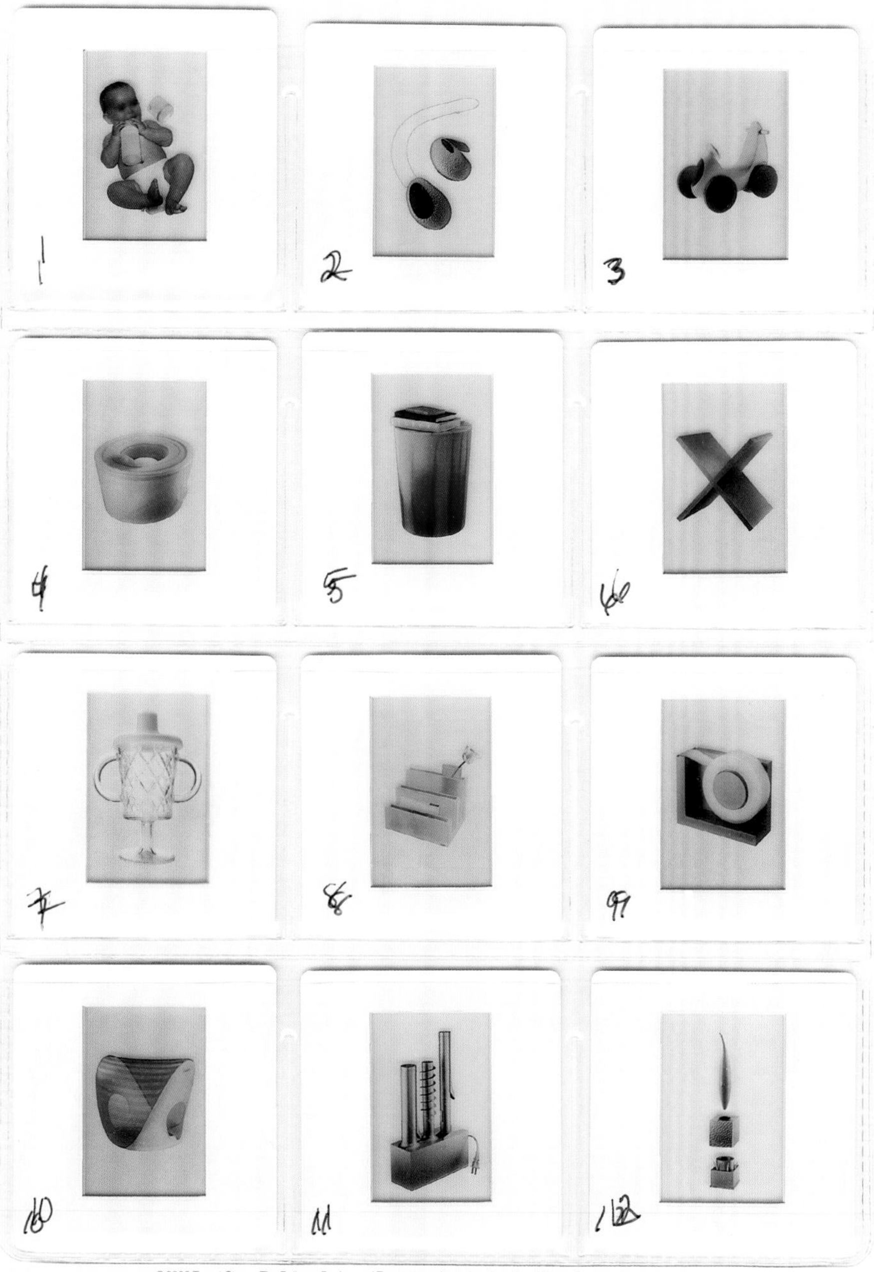

Fast-Forward to the Future with Philippe Starck

Radical democracy is how Philippe Starck takes on the world. The French industrial designer, who has dreamt into reality Tokyo skyscrapers, the private apartments of French President François Mitterrand—plus objects as large as a yacht and as small and innocuous as a folding chair—has done it all with one rigorous mission.
It's simple: take a widely used object, and make it better for the people who use it every day, in look and function. With a resume that includes some of the world's most famous hotels and restaurants, collections with design houses like Kartell and Alessi, and even the first-class lounge of the Eurostar, Starck always begins with one thing—the material—and reimagines how it will reach its greatest utilitarian potential.

Many of Starck's innovations start with an everyday substance—plastic—turned on its head. Think the Louis Ghost armchair, designed for Kartell. The geometric-minded riff is based on a classical Louis XVI design, remade in transparent polycarbonate. It's design fit for royals in a material that's forever fresh.

Starck even brought his radical ideas to bear on a design for Olympic medals, as part of Paris' bid to host the 2024 games. Like us, Starck believes in accessibility, so he created medals that could be divided into four pieces and shared.

"Normally a medal tends to be a sort of witness, a message that says, 'I was there, I did it, I outdid myself. I went beyond myself. I won.' It is extraordinary," said Starck in a video on Twitter. "But today more than ever, the truth is that you're not winning alone. So I wanted this medal to reflect that. If the winner wants to share it, he can share it. It's a really nice way of truly showing team spirit."

We tapped the Frenchman back in 2000 to envision better, brighter versions of household objects: Starck-ian versions of tape dispensers, baby monitors, and magazine racks. He used plastic to create a shape evocative of a fine crystal goblet, but transformed into a spill-proof sippy cup for toddlers. Patrick Douglas, Director of Strategy and Advanced Development, Product Design and Development at Target, worked with Starck closely, and remembers how much he challenged our design and engineering team. "He's a genius," says Douglas. "It's so painstakingly hard to make things look that simple."

Philippe Starck, photographed by Michel Delsol

Opposite: Contact sheet from the Philippe Starck for Target lookbook shoot

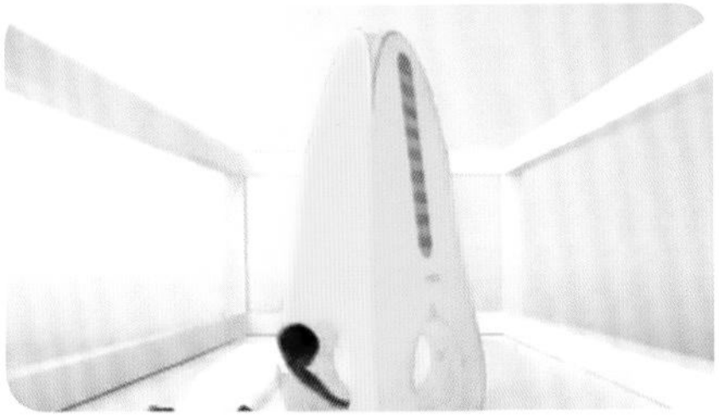

Stills from Philippe Starck for Target TV commercial

Opposite: Cover from Philippe Starck for Target press pack

In Conversation with Philippe Starck

Interview by Michael Bullock

"What is a good object?" a voice ponders in a French accent, before answering its own question. "An object must have emotion, spirit, meaning, love." In 2002, the hyper-charismatic, acclaimed designer Philippe Starck could be found in an unusual place: living rooms dotted all over America, in an unprecedented television commercial for Target. The 30-second spot was rare in that it utilized a designer of significant stature as a spokesman for his own work. In the ad, Starck explains the design philosophies that guided his groundbreaking 51-product Target collaboration, *Starck Reality*.

At that point in his career, the iconoclast was best known for reimagining hotels as surrealist fantasies. Partnered with Studio 54's Ian Schrager, Starck forever altered the trajectory of hotel design—be it the Royalton in New York or the Delano in Miami. Collectively, the properties invented the now-ubiquitous phenomenon of the boutique hotel. In 1996, while in the middle of reinventing the hospitality industry, he took on his own profession—object design—radically challenging how a "serious" designer would present themselves. He appeared topless on the cover of a self-titled monograph, covered in provocative slogans including, "Tomorrow will be less" and "We are mutants." The audacious gesture carried the designer into the territory of pop star—his own image as iconic as the chairs, toothbrushes, and sculptural citrus juicer that had first launched him into stardom. The world-renowned Starck has created everything: from his own line of progressive fragrances to technical prefabricated houses and Steve Jobs' high-profile yacht. Recently, he's expanded his scope beyond our planet. In 2018 he collaborated with space travel company Axiom designing the Habitation Module for their commercial space station. But at the time of the Target collaboration he was most famous for reimagining the hotel as a surrealist fantasy. While Starck cemented his reputation by delivering a refreshing, poetic vision of luxury, he longed to push beyond exclusivity—to execute a vision of design that was accessible to anyone. In the resulting Target commercial, he summed it up expertly: "Target and Starck together, we create design for everyone."

MICHAEL BULLOCK Good morning, Mr. Starck. How was your weekend?
PHILIPPE STARCK My weekend is always like any other day of the week. Today is a good day because I'm in my studio, in Portugal, surrounded by the sea.

MB How does a good day begin?
PS I wake up at 7 a.m. I take a shower that starts off very hot and finishes icy cold because that's good for the brain. At 8 a.m., I'm at my desk—always alone and with good music—looking at the view. Today I see the harbor in front of me. Some fishermen are coming back in with the day's catch, and the waves are as big as buildings.

MB Tell me about your studio.
PS It's a huge room, all in wood, like a Gothic cathedral. It was designed to receive the kings of Italy and Spain. I keep as little as possible on my desk, almost nothing except for my iPad. I have music and that's all. Right now I'm listening to a song titled "Brutal Ardour" by Brian Eno. The album is *Discreet Music*.

MB What are you working on today?
PS We are working on the next International Space Station for Axiom, a private company that collaborates with NASA. It's very interesting to design for life without gravity. I'm also working on my perfume brand. It's beautiful to work on a product that has such little materiality but yet so much power.

My American agent immediately said, “You have to work with Target. They’re the only ones who can develop this vision.”

MB That’s really the full spectrum! Can we go back to the start of the millennium? How did a designer such as yourself come to collaborate with Target—one of the biggest mass-market retailers in the world? At the time, it was an unusual pairing.
PS I’ve spent my life creating the idea of democratic design: offering the highest quality for the lowest price. I was speaking about that with my American agent and he immediately said, “You have to work with Target. They’re the only ones who can develop this vision.” We quickly connected with Target’s president. He didn’t speak like the leader of a huge company. We didn’t speak about business. He spoke with honesty and humanity. He wasn’t cynical. We shared the same values, the same vision. We were two people trying to make the best for our fellow citizens. That’s why I did it.

MB What was the design brief?
PS He gave me a blank page to create whatever I wanted. I took the opportunity to create everything from scratch. It was an incredible amount of work, but I have no fear—I’m a little cuckoo. I took a few tools—my paper pad and pencils—and went to an island off the coast of Africa. I stayed there for 14 days alone. I asked myself: how can I help the Target customer have a better life? I thought specifically about women, people with less money, and children. I designed 51 products, four or five per day, which—if you know the complexity of these things—is completely abnormal. It wasn’t just sketches, it was finding the ideas and vision to design it and make all the technical drawings. I brought finished drawings back to [Target’s headquarters in] Minneapolis, and we started working with the producers.

MB You were quoted at the time as saying, “I don’t need to work … I have made enough for three generations. When I work, it’s for a real political product. It’s for subversion.” Can you elaborate on this?
PS Everything around us influences us. Music, color, architecture, design, cars, art, politics, and fashion. When you are a producer, you have a duty to express what you think, but you also have to take responsibility for what you say. You have to be sure that the influence your objects project [in the world] is the right one for you, but also right for others.

Stills from Philippe Starck for Target TV commercial

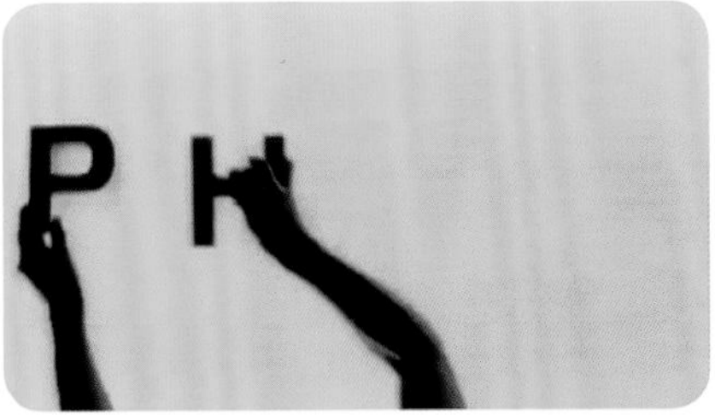

It's more complicated than writing a speech or a song or an article, because it's industry, it's [a] long and heavy [process]. But you can express opinions through objects. A good object is the perfect harmony of the addition of your parameters. These parameters can be the political components: are you making a left-wing or right-wing object? Do you aim to counterbalance the 90% of products made today, which are super macho? There's also an economical aspect: can everybody buy it? Technical aspects: is this the most elegant way to design and build it? An ecological aspect: do people need this product? Have you used the least possible materiality and energy to produce it? And most importantly, are you sure this product will bring a better life to the people who will use it? Are you sure you haven't forgotten to inject love, tenderness, poetry, and humor?

MB There are so many overlapping layers.
PS That's why it's challenging to make an object—it's so difficult to control all these parameters. And [balancing those parameters] is what I tried to do in the Target collection because it was one of the biggest opportunities of my life: the chance to express my vision of what a product should be.

MB Who did you envision as your primary customer?
PS I imagined a single, suburban mother without much money. How could I help her be more elegant with a limited budget when she takes a bottle from her baby bag? It was very important to not only think of her as a mother, but give her the opportunity to feel desirable. I also thought about the children. I didn't want them to feel strange their parents offered them toys but always hid them in [cupboards] when guests visited. The child wonders, "Why is my mother ashamed of my toys?" I tried to make toys that complement the living room or the garden.

MB One of the most unusual pieces is the fancy sippy cup.
PS I've always heard friends referring to their daughters as their "princess." A plastic cup that looks like engraved crystal is a glass a real princess would drink from. I like when [an object] is logical but offers something fun for the same price. That cup is super elegant, like a Chanel perfume bottle.

MB Did you have to change anything about your thought or design process to work at such a large scale?
PS No. No. No! There was no change for me because I always design for a large quantity. To make three chairs priced at $1 million each for three people in the world—it's not right. If you are lucky enough to have a good idea, your duty is to share it with the maximum amount of people.

MB What product did you end up personally using the most?
PS The tape dispenser. The paper knife is also very nice. It's simple. I still have the large bath towel, it's really good. My youngest daughter still uses the toy car.

MB Did the Target project shift the public's perception of your work?
PS Not really—it just expanded my recognition in America and also in museums because many institutions have bought the Target pieces for their design collections. I'm proud of that.

MB I just re-watched the television commercial that advertised the collection. In it you got the rare opportunity to share your design philosophy directly with the public.
PS Ah, yes! It's important to have [your] face on the products. If the public doesn't know the designer, they might not know for sure if they want to buy something. But if you see the face of the guy—and if you have read some interviews—you know if you like him. If you share the same values, you'll feel comfortable to buy and enjoy the objects.

MB Seventeen years later, what impact did Target's collaboration have on your later work?
PS Me? I have not changed. If Target wanted to redo this project again, we would start tomorrow morning because it was very important. My duty is to try to give the right product at the right quality with the right vision at the right price to the most people possible. Target is always in a great position to do that.

S+ARCK

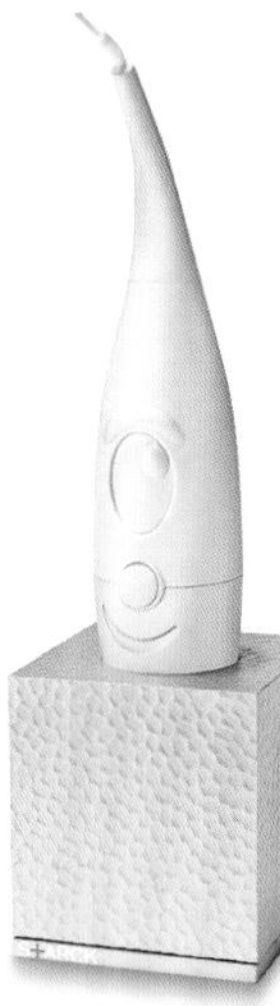

STARCK

This Starck toy was bought by a Target team-member for his son before our collaboration hit shelves, and the designer signed it personally.

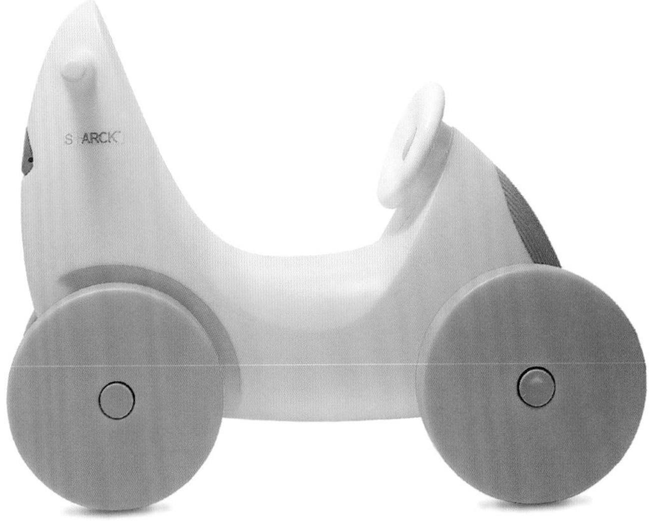

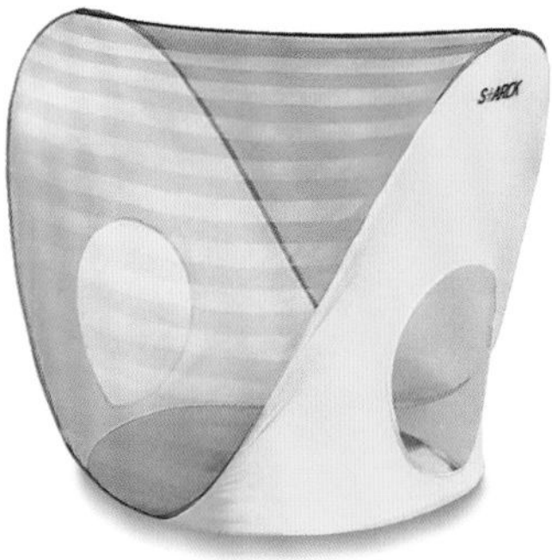

Who knew a curling iron could be counter worthy?

Hunter
2018

Target wanted an innovative launch with a new approach. Since music festivals are in Hunter's DNA, we hosted one for thousands of people in Los Angeles. For those who couldn't be there, we captured content live, broadcasting in real time.

Richard Christiansen
Creative Director, Chandelier Creative

How We Launched Hunter into Its Next Era

Built to last through atmospheric conditions and neverending trend cycles, Hunter boots have been worn by people trotting through the bleakest landscapes since 1856. This includes supermodel Kate Moss, who required a pair of the rain boots to trudge across the Glastonbury fields in 2005. Quickly the footwear became a must for women everywhere.

The rubber rain boot might seem simple in design, but the history of its making is far from it. First imagined by the Duke of Wellington during the Napoleonic Wars, the earliest iterations of the British-named "Wellington boots" were based on riding boots worn by German mercenaries for the British Army. In search of a comfortable shoe his soldiers could wear in battle, the Duke's black Wellingtons—made from leather—were an immediate hit with the British elite.

It was Hunter who saw the potential of a rain boot made from rubber: flexible, strong, easy to splash around in. They were made for soldiers at first too, as a way to protect them in trenches. Coincidentally, the shoe proved ideal for rainy climates—and pretty soon even the Queen of England was spotted in a pair. "The recent development of the Hunter brand has been quite radical," says creative director Alasdhair Willis. "In a relatively short space of time, we have taken the brand's rainboot heritage, renowned for servicing and equipping a traditional British rural country set, and while continuing to engage this very specific customer base have also made Hunter a go-to for a younger global fashion audience." Hunter is at the forefront of an era in which heritage brands have reinvented themselves without sacrificing the durable product that forged their reputation in the first place. It's all about "recognizing our past but always looking to the future," says Willis.

When we met with the ever-inventive brand, a whole new product world was born. Think raincoats, sweatshirts, growlers and hammocks, plus fanny packs made for tourists and club kids alike. To celebrate this launch, we hosted The Ultimate Family Festival—a-free-to-the-public music festival—with an early collection drop and headliners including DJ Questlove, Troye Sivan and Charli XCX. (The latter was outfitted in a head-to-toe glitter suit, with her Hunter for Target rash guard peeking out underneath.) "The day was unforgettable," recalls Laura Cashill, Director of Design Partnerships. "It was a chance to celebrate the limited-edition collection, which is all about fun for the entire family and getting to enjoy the great outdoors, with a festival for all ages that included activities and music performances by some amazing artists—artists that normally sell out the Rose Bowl, but this time it was free and all were invited!"

Above:
In action at The Ultimate Family Festival, staged in partnership with Hunter in LA, 2018

Below:
Charli XCX performs for a crowd. Among the attendees were celebrities from Tiffany Haddish to Kate Bosworth

HUNTER
HUNTER
HUNTER
HUNTER
HUNTER
HUNTER

HUNTER
HUNTER
HUNTER
HUNTER
HUNTER
HUNTER

FE
THE
THE

FEED
2013

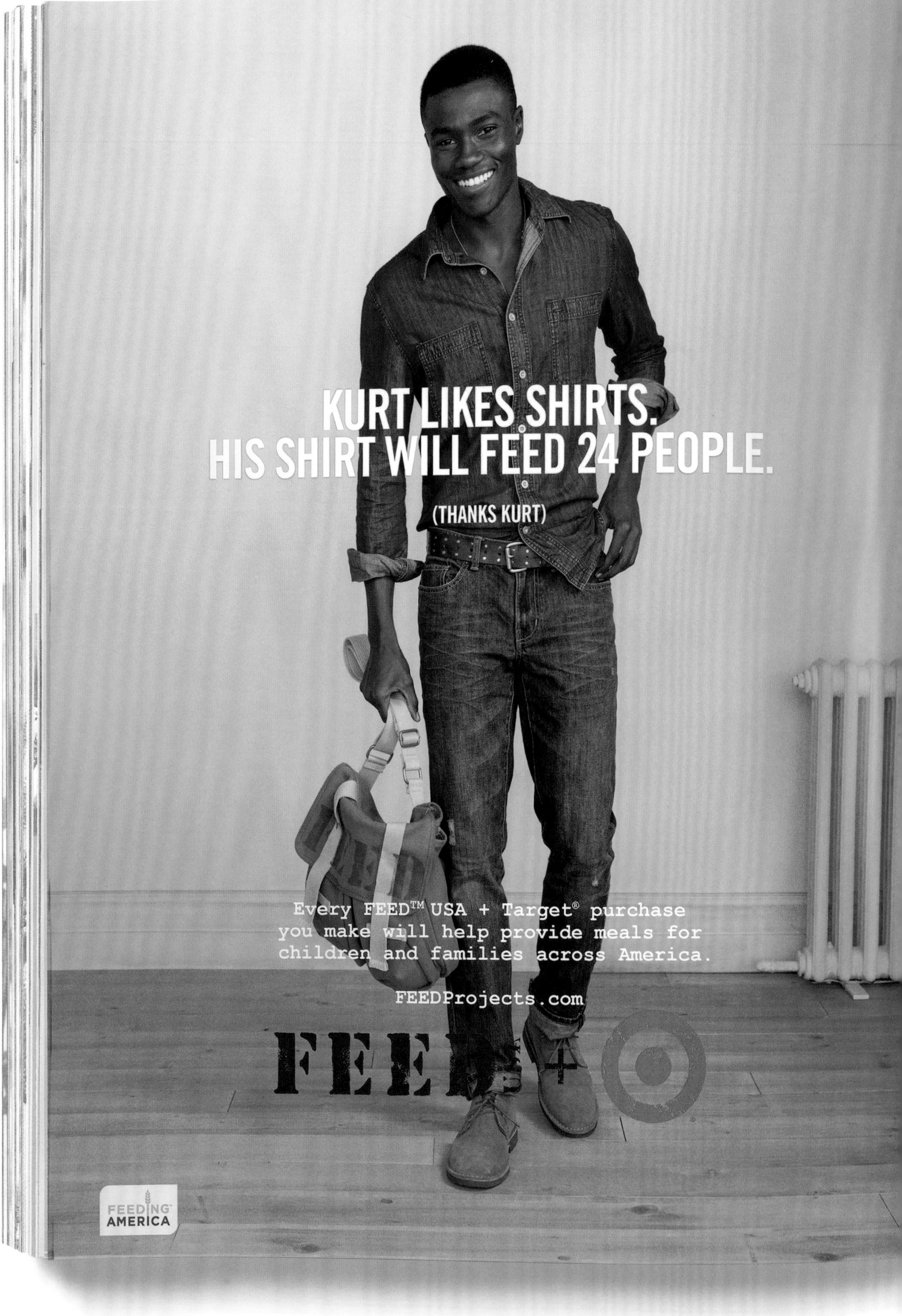
KURT LIKES SHIRTS.
HIS SHIRT WILL FEED 24 PEOPLE.
(THANKS KURT)
Every FEED™ USA + Target® purchase you make will help provide meals for children and families across America.
FEEDProjects.com
FEED +
FEEDING AMERICA

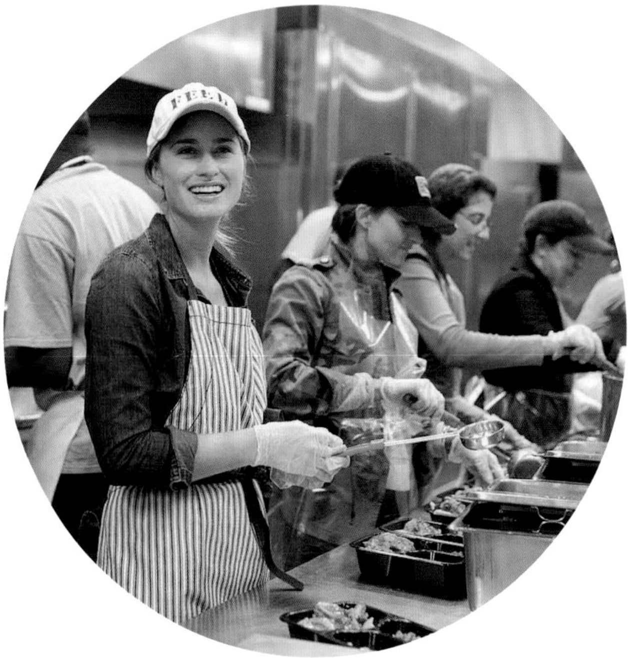

FEED for Thought: On Doing Good with Fashion

Designer Lauren Bush Lauren founded FEED in 2007 after a trip to Guatemala with the World Food Programme exposed her to the extent of chronic malnutrition among the nation's poorest. She hoped to create a company designed for shoppers who "want to put their consumer dollars to good use," as she told *InStyle*. A portion of every sale is donated to FEED's charitable partners, who then distribute meals internationally and across the United States.

FEED specializes in canvas and leather goods—primarily tote bags—with an Americana feel. There's a twist: each FEED product displays the number of meals its purchase generates in charitable donations (some items reveal as many as 185). Items are emblazoned with slogans like "WOMAN ON A MISSION" and "FEED THE CHILDREN OF THE WORLD."

In 2013, we partnered with FEED, expanding the then-bag-only brand to build a collection of home products, sporting goods, stationery and apparel. "As the founder of FEED, I am passionate about the fight against hunger," said Lauren Bush Lauren at the time. "Through product sales, we hope to provide 10 million meals to Americans in need, which would make it the largest US initiative in FEED's history."

Over the past two decades, Americans have grown increasingly interested in linking their philanthropic efforts with their personal style, whether they're buying slogan tees and totes or seeking out brands that use sustainable materials. FEED has been at the forefront of this movement, using clever branding to transform giving into a lifestyle signifier, and raising huge amounts of money for charity in the process. It's a win-win.

Photograph courtesy Lauren Bush Lauren

Opposite: FEED + Target campaign photographed by Mei Tao

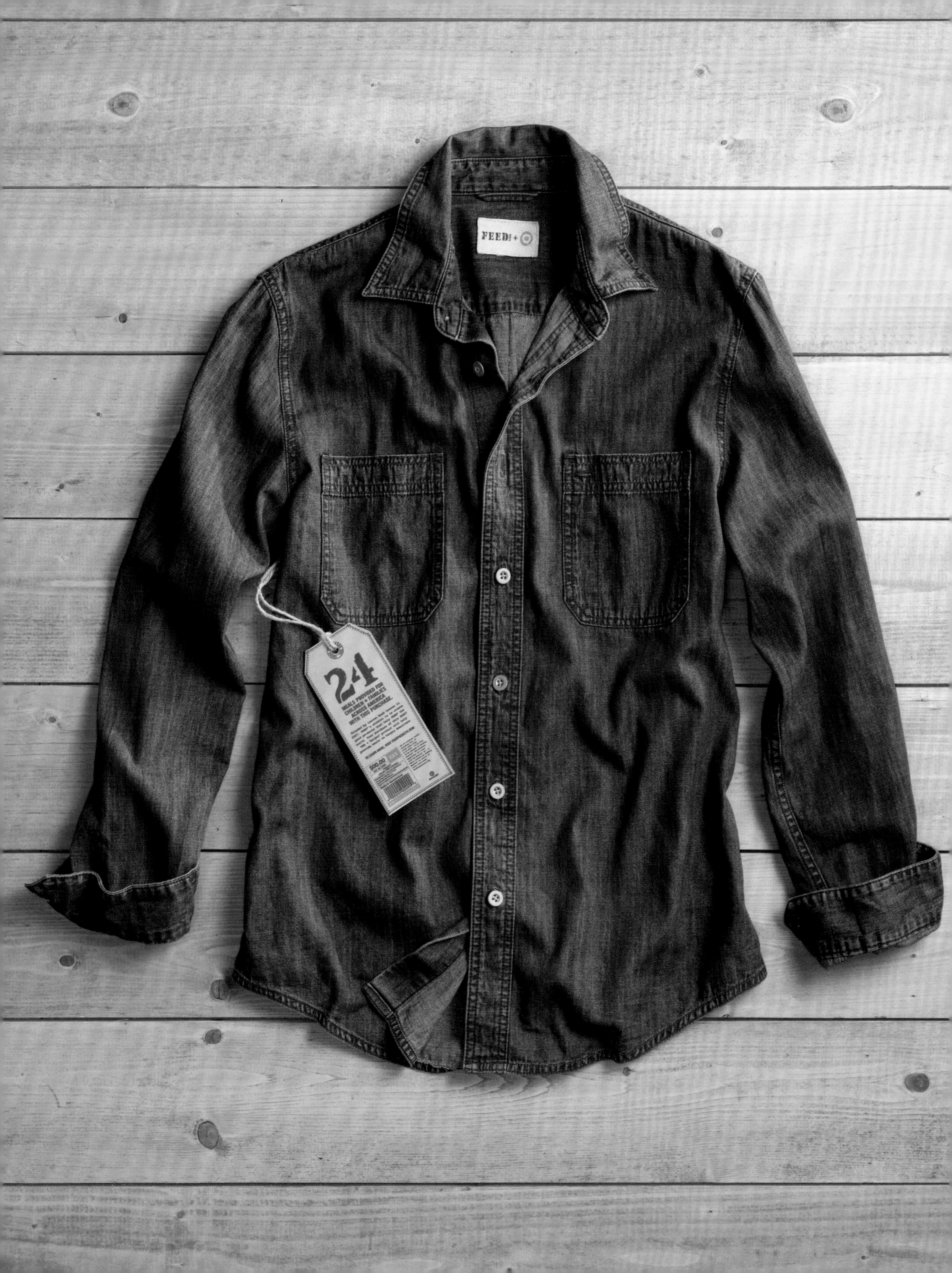
FEED
24
MEALS PROVIDED FOR
CHILDREN + FAMILIES
ACROSS AMERICA
WITH THIS PURCHASE.
$00.00

A selection of items from the 50-plus piece FEED + Target collection

Target Guest
AMOXICILLIN 500MG
Generic For:
Mfr:
Take one (1) capsule by mouth two (2) times a day for ten days.
Qty:
Refill:
Dr. C Williams
Thru:
Drug Exp:
Qty Rem:
Disp:
C Williams
Orig:
NDC:
NSC Capsule
Rx:
(877) 798-2743
TARGET PHARMACY

Deborah
Adler
2005-2015

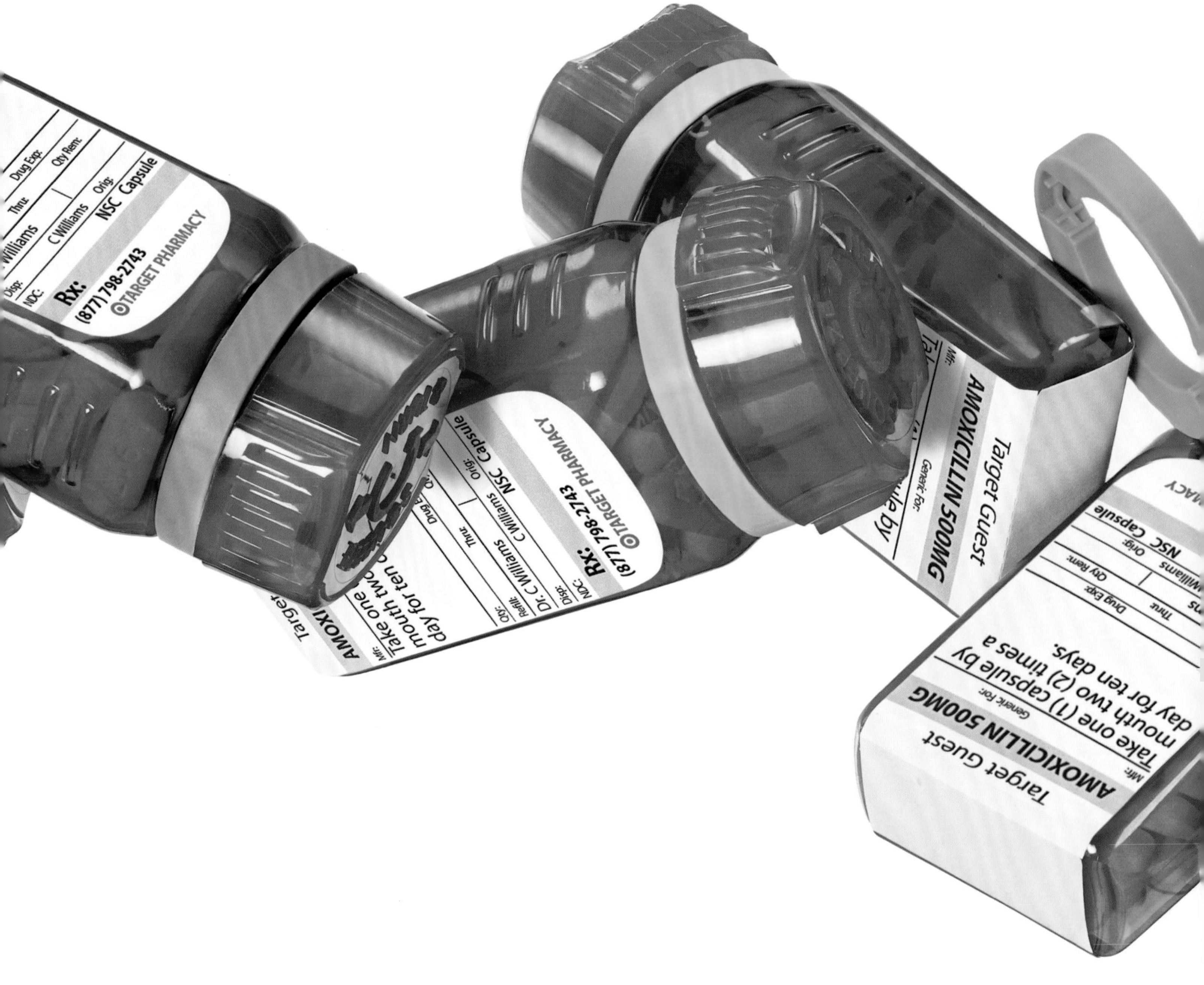

The fastest way into the world was through a national pharmacy. That's when I contacted Target. Using design as a differentiator was at the core of their brand, and I knew they'd be willing to take a risk with this sort of innovation.

Inspired by Grandma Helen. After her grandmother accidentally took her grandfather's medicine, designer Deborah Adler partnered with Target to create a better way to take medicine.
Commended by:
Home Safety Council
Institute of Safe Medication Practices
Time Magazine
U.S. Surgeon General
Easy-to-read label with larger type and simple instructions
Helen Adler
AMOXICILLIN 250MG
Capsule
Generic for: Amoxil
Take one capsule by mouth three times daily until gone
qty: 30
refills: No
Dr. C Wilson
disp: 03/21/06 TST
mfr:
NDC: 00781-2020-05
(877)798-2743
6666067-1375
TARGET PHARMACY
900 Nicollet Mall
Minneapolis, MN 55403
PATIENT INFO CARD
Attached info card with important personal and drug information
Custom-color ID ring for each member of the family
ClearRx.℠ A prescription system that simplifies, informs and personalizes medications.
This innovative system includes color-coded ID rings, an easy-to-read label and an attached patient information card, giving seniors and everyone else a little extra dose of certainty. It's easy to transfer your prescriptions in store, on-line at Target.com or call 1-877-RX-TARGET. Exclusively at Target Pharmacy.

Deborah Adler stands with her grandmother, Helen, alongside Adler's ClearRx bottle

In Conversation with Deborah Adler

Interview by Jill Singer

There aren't many designers who get to see the project they developed in art school acquired for the permanent collection at New York's Museum of Modern Art. But that's exactly what happened to Deborah Adler, who redesigned the humble pill bottle as a thesis project at New York's School of Visual Arts (SVA), only to have it picked up a few years later by Target for use across their in-store pharmacies nationally. The now-iconic red drugstore bottle, which came to be known as ClearRx, was celebrated for its flat, readable surface, its color-coded rings to avoid family mix-ups, and digestible hierarchy of information. The Industrial Design Society of America named it America's Design of the Decade. But even more, it changed the lives—and possibly medical outcomes—for countless of patients and, with it, the conversation around patient care.

JILL SINGER Tell me about how you came to design as a career. Was it something you were interested in as a kid?
DEBORAH ADLER Growing up, I loved the arts and I loved painting. I wasn't even sure what design was at the time, so when I went to the University of Vermont for my undergrad, I was a Fine Arts major. When I graduated from college, I got a job as an intern in a small graphic design studio run by an SVA grad. I started learning about design there. I found that I was really good with programs like FreeHand and Photoshop, but that I was missing certain things—context, history, typography. So I applied to SVA, to an MFA Design program called the "Designer as Author and Entrepreneur." That's sort of what changed my whole life in terms of seeing [the world] through the lens of a designer. I also grew up in a family of doctors. My dad was a doctor, my mom was a nurse, my grandfather was a doctor, my uncle's a doctor—and as a young girl, I aspired to be like them in some way, to try and make a difference. I think that design met health in a really powerful way for me when I was getting my master's.

JS It's interesting that you did a "Designer as Author and Entrepreneur" program. That kind of program is popular now, but the idea that a designer ought to be a businessperson as well was relatively new back then.
DA Yes, and design for social good wasn't very popular back then either! The program was only two years old at the time, and as a student, I'd flip through old design books from the two previous years. One student had designed a system making it easier for pilots to land planes on runways; another had designed tags that people with vision trouble could apply to their clothes to see what color they were wearing. I was really inspired by that, and I wanted to come up with something that would make a real difference in people's lives. I guess I also just have an entrepreneurial spirit. It's in me. I'm ambitious, and I think big.

JS What inspired your thesis project, SafeRx—the project that eventually led you to Target?
DA In my SVA program, you had to come up with an idea you could eventually bring to market. At first, I had this idea to design a mecca for people with curly hair. I wanted to come up with a line of products that would speak to different cultures, so an African American curl versus an Eastern European curl. But then the Twin Towers fell, and suddenly my curly hair idea seemed really silly. Around the same time, I was at my grandparents' house, and my grandmother accidentally took my grandfather's medication. They had both been prescribed the same drug, but different dosage strengths. Their initials are the same. Her name was Helen, his name was Herman. H. Adler. When I looked inside their medicine cabinet, I was not at all surprised that the error occurred. Their pill bottles were practically identical. As a granddaughter, I was concerned for their health, but as a designer, I saw an urgent problem that needed to be solved, and that's sort of what set my light bulb off.

JS What needed fixing?
DA I started to dig a bit deeper and realized that my grandparents were not alone. Half of us don't take our prescriptions correctly. That could be anything from taking two Advil instead of one to really mixing up complex drug regimens. That leads to poor adherence, which leads to horrible outcomes, which leads to readmissions to hospitals, and so on. I realized that coming up with a system that was simpler to use would [not only] be good for my grandma, but a lot of other people. No one had really considered the redesign of a pill bottle before. I started to develop a system that changed the shape of the bottle, included color coding, and reorganized the hierarchy of information, so that the drug name was at the top, not tucked away at the bottom. You could see a million mistakes when you looked through a medicine cabinet.

JS How did Target get involved?
DA For my thesis, I designed all of these little prototypes. I went down to Canal Street Plastics to get tubing, bought dollhouse materials—like tiny L-shaped brackets—and I made really good imitations of pill bottles. I made the bottles D-shaped, so I cut pill caps in half, and then I put the drug information in [the] back so that it slid in and out of the L-shaped bracket. I also included a magnifying lens, and built this huge medicine cabinet. After I showed my thesis, I decided I would bring it to Washington, DC, to show it to the Food and Drug Administration.

I saw an urgent problem that needed to be solved, and that's sort of what set my light bulb off.

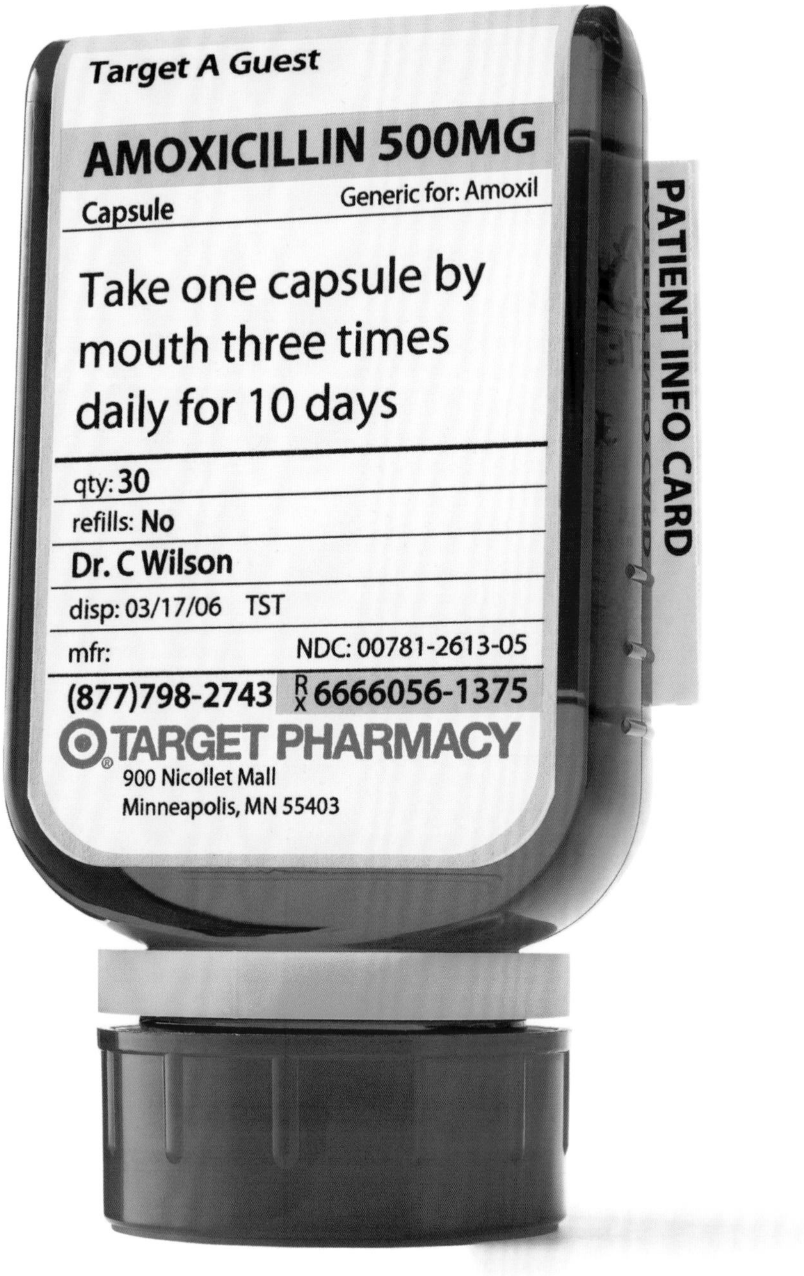

Target A Guest
AMOXICILLIN 500MG
Capsule
Generic for: Amoxil
Take one capsule by mouth three times daily for 10 days
qty: 30
refills: No
Dr. C Wilson
disp: 03/17/06 TST
mfr:
NDC: 00781-2613-05
(877)798-2743
Rx 6666056-1375
TARGET PHARMACY
900 Nicollet Mall
Minneapolis, MN 55403
PATIENT INFO CARD

ClearRx bottle. The color-coded rings helped identify who the pills belong to, in an effort to reduce medication related mistakes

I had high hopes of making it a Federal standard, and when I met with the FDA, they were excited by the idea, too. But their hands were tied because each state has its own Board of Pharmacy. I quickly realized the fastest way into the world was through a national pharmacy—that's when I contacted Target. Using design as a differentiator was at the core of their brand, and I knew they'd be willing to take a risk with this sort of innovation. I should say that when I first graduated, I went to Milton Glaser's studio—I had taken a class with him—and asked if I could show him my thesis. He loved it. I asked him for a job. He said no, and I went to work at Kiehl's. I got a call six months later saying Milton wanted to meet with me, so I went to his studio. He hired me, and I worked there for six years. We were in a taxi one day, and he said to me, "You know, I really want to see this happen in my lifetime"—my thesis project, that is. When he said that, I suddenly regained confidence. I emailed Minda Gralnek, who was creative director at Target at the time, and I cc'd Milton, which I think gave me a lot of credibility. They came to New York, we showed them the idea, and they said, "We need you to come out to Target." Milton came with me and introduced the project, which was really something. The next thing I know, Target took me and my idea under their wing and we launched ClearRx.

JS How did the project change from its original conception to when Target launched it in the marketplace?
DA When Target decided to move forward, I quickly learned that my prototypes would not function. They wanted to get it into the world really fast, so the cap had to fit on a round neck, or else they'd have to go through child-safety testing. They paired me with an industrial designer, Klaus Rosberg, and we designed a new bottle with a round neck. The color-coding also changed. They didn't have color printers, so we had to add colored rings around the neck of each bottle to indicate which person in your household each pill belonged to. I also got to redesign the warning icons. We came up with little pictograms for 30 or 40 different warnings—"Do not take this medicine on an empty stomach," "Do not chew." Milton got to work on that with me, so that was a lot of fun. We did "do not drive while intoxicated," and it was a car just driving straight into a wall.

JS I didn't realize what a fairy godfather figure Milton Glaser was for you. What else did you learn from him?
DA One of the biggest things was how to handle not finding a solution. I tend to be more anxious—if I don't know the answer to a design problem, I rush to find it. He would always say, "When the pieces of the puzzle aren't fitting together is when you are the most fertile." If you're smart, you'll stay in that space for as long as you can because that's where things unfold and the magic happens. It's helped me a million times in my career.

JS With ClearRx, did the issue of sustainability ever come up? People are always going to trash their pill bottles.
DA I don't even know how far they made it, but we did try. It's not just about my grandma, it's about my great-grandchildren—and it's not just people, it's the world. I get how health expands to our whole planet. I think that's a huge problem that has to be dealt with right now.

JS Did the Target project change the focus of your practice to medicine?
DA I focus on innovation in health and beauty—whether it be a brand identity system for a skincare line to a Foley catheter tray that reduces the incidence of urinary tract infections to an app for families who suffer from severe food allergies. We do a lot of work in health and hospital systems.

JS How do you come up with ideas when they aren't directives from other companies? Where do you find inspiration?
DA I can't believe I didn't mention my *gemba*! The *gemba* is a Japanese term. Toyota pioneered it in Japan with their "lean manufacturing" process. They wanted to come up with more efficient ways to make cars, so they put the driver at the center. The healthcare community became very interested in this process because they wanted to try and reduce the incidence of heart attacks. They went to Japan and were so inspired that a couple of health systems brought this practice back to the healthcare communities. Gemba basically means "the real place." It says that you have to go to the place where the work is done to see the steps that lead into a larger action. For my grandmother, the Gemba was her medicine cabinet. For a surgeon, it's the table where he's performing surgery. For a nurse, it's the patient's bedside. Wherever it is, you have to put yourself in the shoes of the person to figure out what would they do, and what would they need next. It's funny, because the Target slogan was "Design for All." I love the idea of design for all, but I don't think that means design for the world. I think you need to start with the person. Design for the person, and then that will translate to all.

JS What was the response like when ClearRx got out to the world, and you were the face behind it? Weren't you in a commercial with Michael Graves?
DA I don't think any of us, Target or myself, were expecting the overwhelming response. But I also think ClearRx gave people hope that at the end of the day, they were being thought of. Before, nobody thought about the patient when it came to that pill bottle. It was just about operations, and getting the right pill in the right vial, with the right labeling [on the production end.] And yes, that's important, but it's not important if the patient doesn't understand what they're doing. I'll never forget when we were beta testing the product in one of the first [Target] pharmacies. It was in Florida, and this pharmacist named Patrick was dispensing the medication into the new bottle with the new label for the first time. That's when I realized something that began as a student project was now so much bigger than me. It was something Patrick was taking ownership of, and rightfully so, because he's on the front lines. If he doesn't do it right, the whole thing falls apart. So, I think everyone was very happy. I got a letter from the Surgeon General commending me—and Target. It was a real moment. But honestly, we've just scratched the surface in terms of trying to change healthcare and be a force in that space. That's where I'm headed, and I am very grateful that I had Target for that experience.

TOMS
2014
TOMS

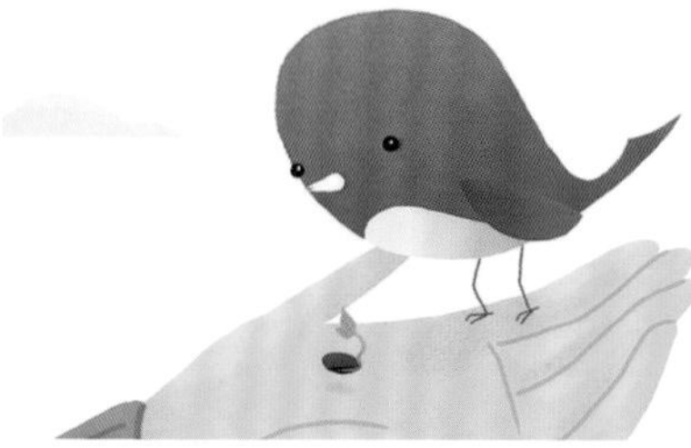

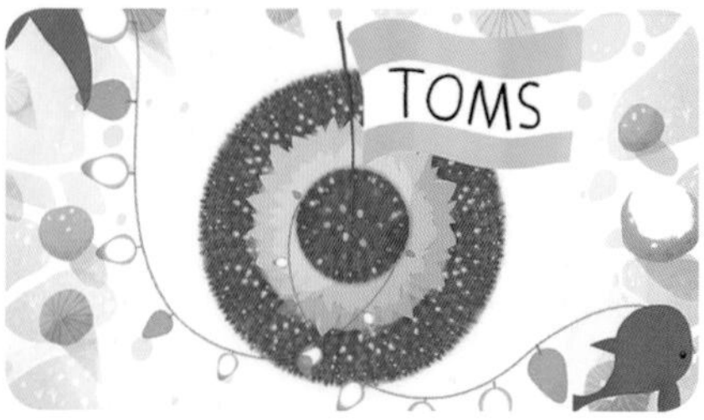

TOMS pioneered the “one for one” model. But here, we had to give back in new ways with new products. *The Giving Tree* was a great metaphor for the TOMS and Target story, brought to life with animation. Blake Mycoskie planted a tree, supplying blankets, clothing and food.

Richard Christiansen
Creative Director, Chandelier Creative

With TOMS, We Brought One For One to More

In 2002, entrepreneur Blake Mycoskie traveled to Argentina as a contestant on *The Amazing Race*, and was struck by the alpargata espadrilles he saw locals wearing. In 2006, he launched TOMS, a footwear company with a unique charity angle: the company donated one pair of canvas slip-ons to people in developing countries for each pair sold. Eventually, TOMS expanded into eyewear, bags, coffee, and more—always giving back a related product or service with each sale. The company has offered shoes, vision health, clean water, safe birth, and bullying prevention services to millions of people worldwide.

But TOMS isn't just a charity enterprise—it's also an influential and profitable clothing company with sharp design and a clear point of view. TOMS shoes have one of the most recognizable footwear silhouettes of the past 20 years, as ubiquitous as they are simple. In 2014, we collaborated with their seminal design team for the holidays, expanding their wares beyond shoes to include home goods and apparel. Every purchase was matched by a donation of a blanket through the Red Cross or a week of meals via Feeding America and Food Banks Canada. Shoes were also donated, via TOMS' established channels.

The partnership culminated in a surprising viral moment. "We wanted to bring people together, because that's what the holidays are all about," says Noria Morales, Senior Director of Influencer and Brand Collaborations at Target. Taking the idea of community quite literally, Target and TOMS created the Together Sweater, a fantastical wool garment with multiple head-holes designed to be worn by several people at once. Ranging in scale from two heads to six, they transformed their wearers into a single many-limbed organism, like something out of a Dr. Seuss book. The sweater turned into a phenomenon after Ellen DeGeneres featured it on her talk show, inviting 12 audience members to wear two six-person sweaters and compete in the "sweater game," where they frantically tried to throw washcloths into buckets; of course, each team of six only had two usable arms apiece, and hijinks ensued. The segment was a hit, and people around the world began taking photos with their pets and family members sharing the sweater; two-thirds of Boyz II Men even appeared in one.

"None of those people who wore the sweater were paid partnerships," emphasizes Morales. "Everyone just loved how fun it was. It was all about the joy of the holidays and the togetherness, so people jumped right in."

Blake Mycoskie in Malaysia, courtesy TOMS Malaysia

Opposite: Stills from TOMS for Target TV commercial

ONE FOR ONE, FOR ALL

A selection of items from the 50-plus piece TOMS for Target collection

Opposite: Campaign photographed by Tom Schirmacher

Tord
Boontje
2006

Tord Boontje's Immersive Winter Wonderland

Swans, a reindeer, a horse, a dog, an owl, a rabbit and a llama: these are just some of the animals that appear in a series of dream-like 2006 holiday commercials by Tord Boontje for Target. All of them are snow white. Goldfrapp's dream-pop anthem "Fly Me Away" plays as a father and son enjoy a meal in a candle-lit snowscape. An enigmatic man in a suit sits on a log, a thosand-watt smile lighting up his face, as he intones, in a cheerful Scandinavian accent, "My name is Tord Boontje. I've created a magical world for you. Come celebrate the season with me."

The ad's wintry palette (midnight blues and crisp white), animal cameos, and fantastical tone embodied the seasonal experience crafted by Boontje, a celebrated industrial designer from the Netherlands. "I always start designing by asking myself, what would I really like to live with," he said. "In this case, it led to objects which are either great gifts or that can bring wonder and fantasy into everyone's home and create a very festive, warm, romantic atmosphere; a house filled with illumination and good feelings." The emotions he evoked may be traditional, but his execution was not—look no further than a mind-bending, spiky candelabra made from clear red plastic, or the plates embossed with intricate patterns resembling lace tracery. That linework echoed across the collection, appearing on cups, napkins, and delicate paper ornaments. Boontje even designed clear plastic gift cards decorated with silhouettes of reindeer and snowflakes.

And he didn't just deliver a line of home goods. Boontje's studio created environments for 1,400 of our stores and art-directed the campaign's commercials and photography. The end result was the most comprehensive collaboration we've ever commissioned—an inviting winter wonderland in every sense of the word.

Candelabra from the 35-piece Tord Boontje for Target collection

Opposite: Stills from Tord Boontje for Target TV commercial

Dwell Magazine
2016-2017

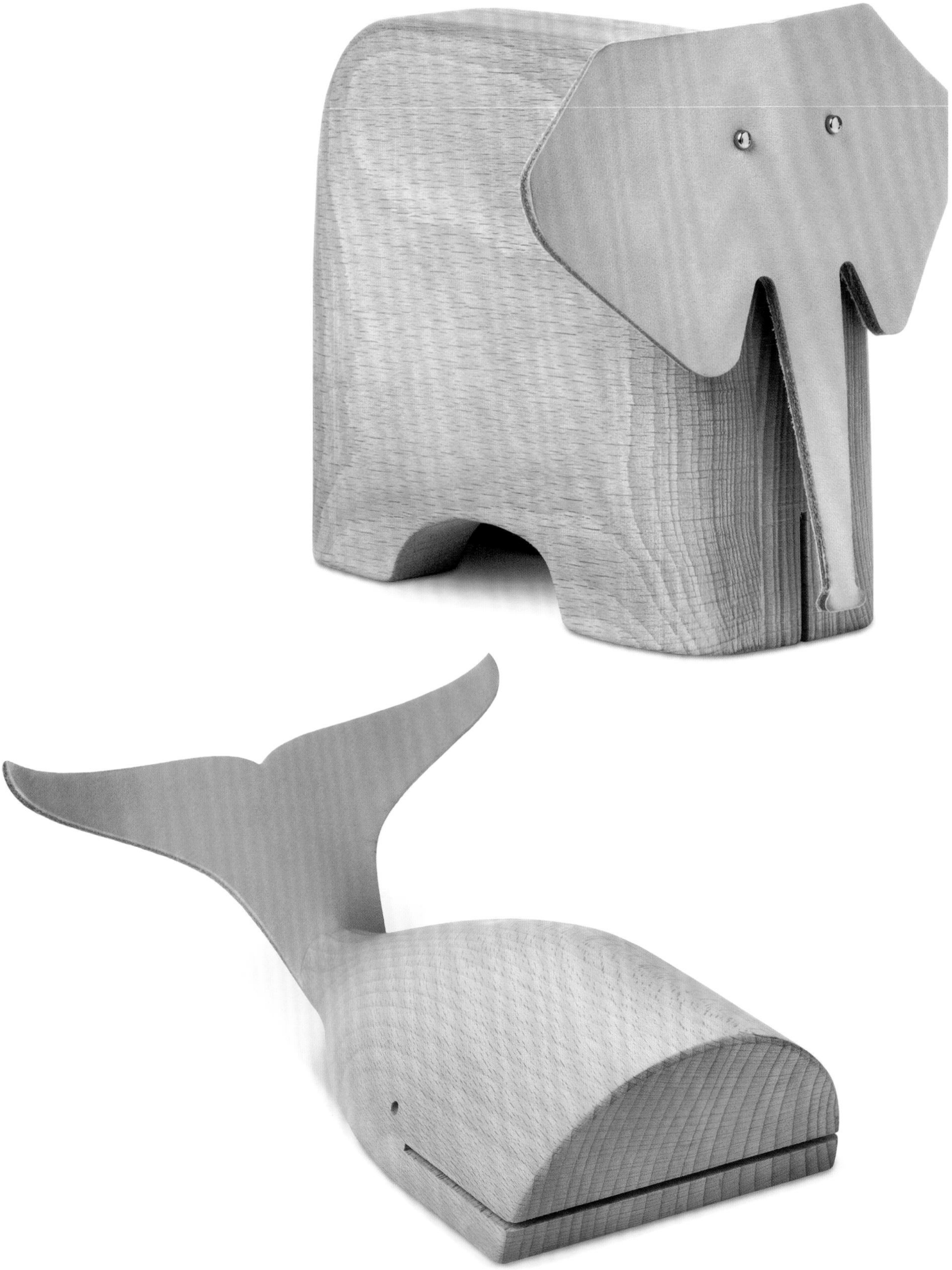

Alexander Girard

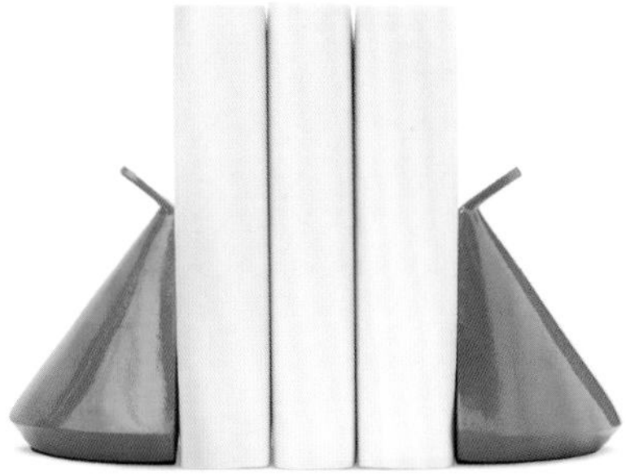

Harmonious Home Interiors with Dwell Magazine

Dwell believes in bringing modern design to the masses—and so do we. Founded in 2000, it's a media company (read: a magazine about living well, no matter who you are) and a platform aimed at connecting designers, architects and admirers. Their goal is simple: create an environment that's conducive to good design. Knowing our guests are interested in making their home a nest, the concept behind our partnership came naturally: a sprawling, 125-plus-piece furniture and home accessories line made for easy mix-and-matching with a friendly modernist feel.

The collection was designed by Chris Deam and Nick Dine, of the firm Deam + Dine, in partnership with our team—we put our heads together to craft a series of pieces that felt at once clean and warm. It often came down to the smallest details, like rounding off the edges of trays, chairs and table legs. From sleek chairs with extended shelves for feet to rest easy on, to clean white clocks and tiny, wall-hanging mirrors, every item was designed to fit with ease into small spaces. They were lightweight and slim as well: perfect for people always on the move.

As always, we worked with partners who believed in making beautiful design accessible. "So often, good design or design-driven product is out of reach to the regular consumer," said Dine. "I see these pieces living comfortably in any home," he continued. "We want people who are just starting out or have an established home to be able to integrate our work."

Clean, curved lines and pared-back details abound in the collection by Dwell Magazine, for Target

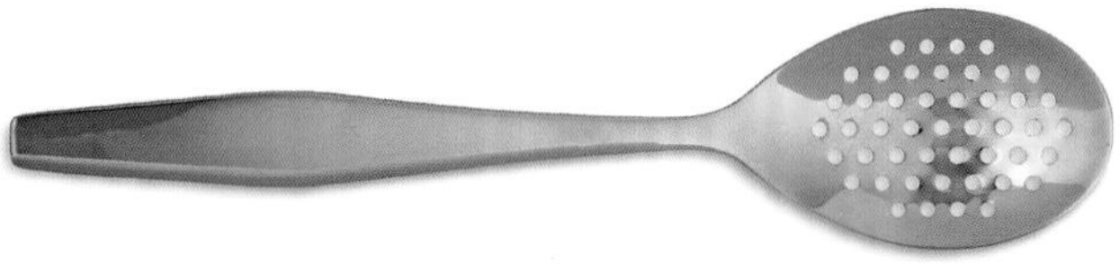

To inform their mid-century designs, Deam + Dine visited homes of everyday Americans, getting feedback on how they live.

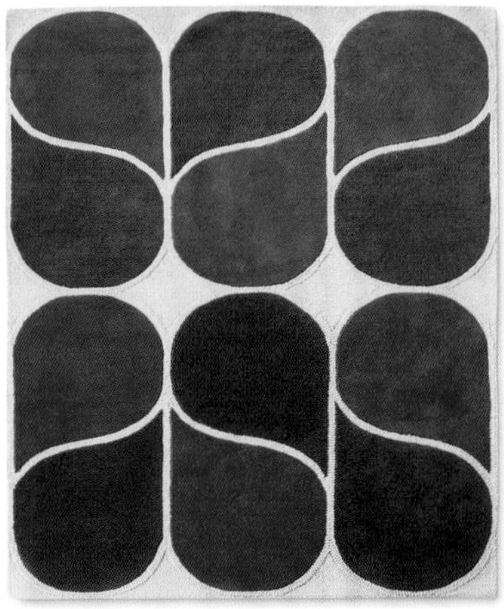

Daisies dance across dresses, their centers dyed an unreal blue. Wild, abstracted petals are splashed across dinner plates and rain boots, sometimes climbing along bicycle handlebars. The world's most famous jagged line, a multicolored Missoni zigzag, joyfully wraps its way around a 400-piece collection: towels, bedding, makeup bags and silky scarves. In the world of these print-loving designers, life as we know it becomes a visual feast, an ever-changing work of art.

Missoni
2011

Liberty London
2010

Lilly Pulitzer
2015

Marimekko
2016

Peter Pilotto
2014

Thakoon
2008

Prabal Gurung
2013

Maximalists

Missoni
2011

Missoni Zigzags Into America

Spontaneity and self-expression have always been part of Missoni's DNA. Now headquartered in Varese, Northern Italy, the poptastic, zigzaggy fashion house began quite by accident—with the meeting of two lovers in 1948. Back then, Ottavio "Tai" Missoni was competing as a hurdler in the London Summer Olympics; his specialty was the 400-meter race. It was there he met Rosita, who he married soon after, and together the pair forged a creative bond. In interviews, she remembered her husband's outfit when meeting up post-Games in Piccadilly Circus. He wore an "elegant knit tie" and the Italian coat of arms on his electric blue jacket.

At the time, Tai was already making sporty daywear with his teammate: knitted tracksuits with then-radical zippers zooming up the legs. In 1967, he debuted a collection of sporty Lurex dresses on the runway with Rosita—the show was staged at the Palazzo Pitti in Florence. Missoni's next show, the same year, was set at a Milanese swimming pool with a blow-up house in the middle. When the house collapsed unexpectedly, Missoni's models threw a pool party.

That effortless, can't-be-staged formula has never left the brand—and that's exactly why we wanted in. For our partnership, zigzags, sharp stripes and mod-like swirling forms shot across everything imaginable: bedspreads, bicycles—even wine boxes. There were 400 made-just-for-Target products, and many sold out in 24 hours.

Ottavio Missoni with his daughter Angela, Giuseppe Pino/Mondadori Portfolio, 1968

Opposite: A model in full Missoni poses on Missoni pillows, courtesy Hulton Archive, 1975

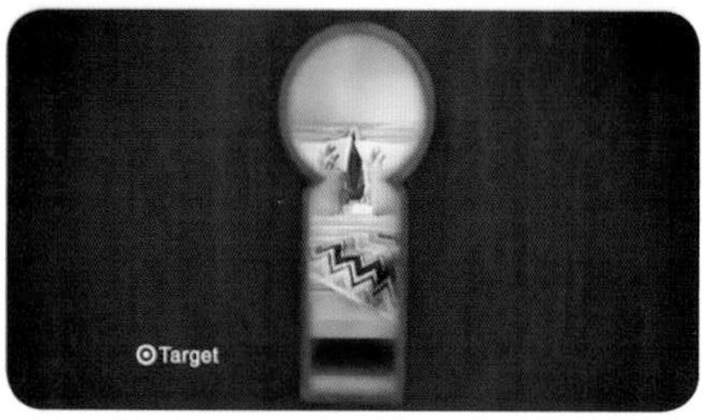

Before it even reached stores, the Missoni partnership was madness. During the shooting of our campaign film in Milan—starring Margherita Maccapani Missoni, granddaughter of the founders—the team was swarmed by Italian paparazzi, right outside the Duomo. "I've been on a lot of on-location sets, but the Italian paparazzi were something new for me!" remembers Laura Cashill, Director of Design Partnerships. "I thought, 'Is this all because of Margherita?' Turns out we also had a lot of Italian actors in our cast, but had no idea how incredibly popular they were!"

The World's Biggest Blogger Kick-starts Missoni Madness

Released amid the mayhem of New York Fashion Week, our Missoni launch featured a radical, dreamlike blogger named Little Marina. When she made her online debut, it seemed she might be real—she blogged and tweeted from her home in Northern Italy, hyping up the collaboration like any aspiring fashion starlet. But at our celeb-dotted party in NYC, her identity was finally unveiled. Little Marina was a gigantic, 25-foot doll-turned-robot, dressed in full Missoni for Target—a fitting guest of honor for one of our biggest-ever launches. She held a supersized smartphone and colossal business cards, which she'd hand out to unsuspecting guests. Brought to life "beyond the shelf" by an Academy Award-winning character effects studio, Little Marina exuded glamour in spades—but behind the scenes it was a little different. Her size meant she was carted around New York on an open-bed trailer, making meet-and-greet cameos at Bryant Park, Lincoln Center and blogger conferences.

Later, when the collection reached stores, the Missoni fever kick-started by Little Marina enveloped guests across the country. There were reports of around-the-block lines on launch day in multiple cities. Superfan Samantha Stewart found her local Target empty, then drove to two more to get her Missoni fix. "As you can see," she shared online at the time, "my 'controlled' excitement did not stay that way!"

Little Marina in New York, photographed by Bryan Derballa

Opposite: Stills from the Missoni for Target TV commercial

The term "fiammata" refers to Missoni's angular zigzag knit—taken from the Italian word for flame.

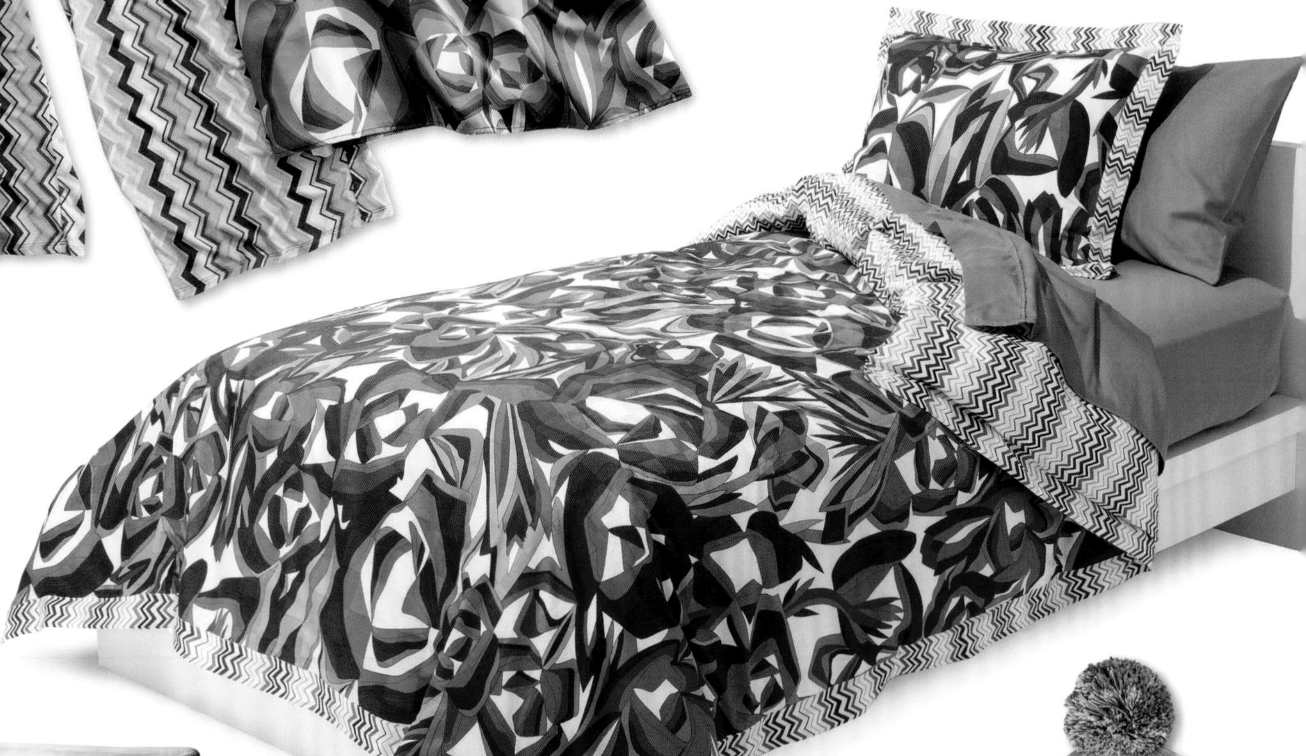

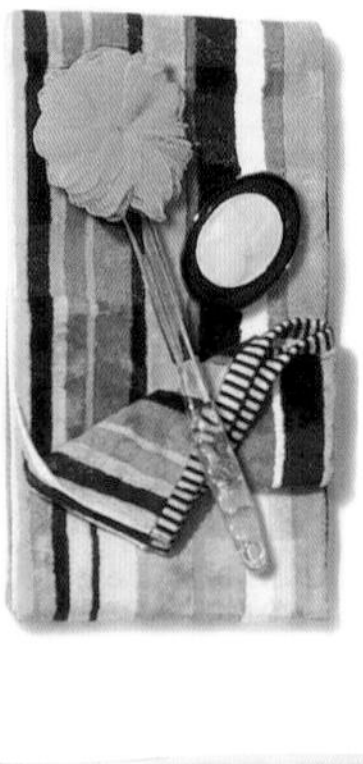

Based on 60s fashion caper films, our collection gave fresh twists to archival Missoni patterns.

Liberty
London
2010

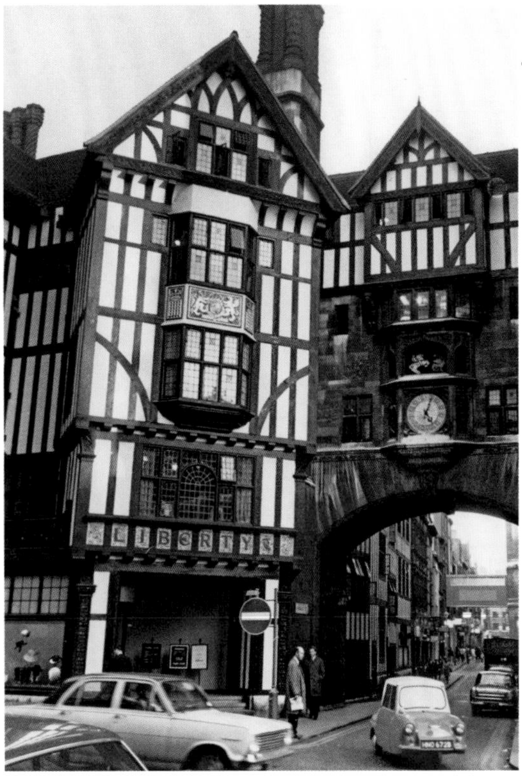

From Bowie to Bullseye: The Psychedelic Plasticity of Liberty Prints

Founder of the London department store—and print house—of the same name, Arthur Lasenby Liberty began selling fabrics at age 16 with his uncle. In 1875, he set up a London storefront of his own, calling it Liberty & Co.—and counted Oscar Wilde among his earliest fans. A few decades later, one of Liberty's buyers was traveling through the Ethiopian highlands close to Lake Tana when he stumbled upon some curious silky fibers. Once transported to England, the ultra-fine cotton yarns were woven into a series of textiles and screen-printed by Liberty. Not only did Tana Lawn become one of the store's most popular fabrics— beloved for its silky, luxurious feel—but it was a favorite of designers for its hand-drawn and painted patterns: from paisleys to psychedelic-inflected Art Nouveau shapes.

With their distinctive, kaleidoscopic prints, Liberty fabrics quickly became a staple of the 60s and 70s rock 'n' roll set, including miniskirt inventor and Mod Queen Mary Quant. Yves Saint Laurent made his first maxi dress from Liberty's Macedonia pattern, and disruptor David Bowie—the High Priest of Pop—wore Liberty on the album cover of *The Rise and Fall of Ziggy Stardust and the Spiders from Mars*. In 1994, designer Vivienne Westwood confirmed Liberty's continued reign of cool, sending supermodels like Karen Mulder and Naomi Campbell down her radical punk-meets-Victoriana runway in its prints.

In 2010, we joined forces with the famed London department store, at the height of the mix-and-match print trend. Liberty's flower power patterns exploded across dresses, bedding, utensils and garden tools for Target—even a bright pink bicycle—ready for a new guard of bohemian tastemakers to make the prints their own.

Liberty & Co's store-front, photographed by Chris Ratcliffe/ Bloomberg

Opposite: David Bowie performs at the Aylesbury Friars while decked out in Liberty prints, 1972

I moved from the UK to Florida years ago—and while I don't miss the weather, I miss Liberty London! Their prints are so rich and perfectly English. I was so excited when Target launched their Liberty line. They had a few products I'd never seen before, so I bought every tea set I could get my hands on, plus a stack of colorful trays for Sunday morning breakfasts in bed. It was so fun to see my friends go wild over it as well—it was all new to them but felt just like home to me.

Lucy Harrogate, Liberty London fan

Larger-than-life products appear in the Liberty London for Target TV commercial

Prints were hand-wrapped around bicycles—only perfected by two manufacturers worldwide.

LIBERTY

Lilly

Lilly
Pulitzer
2015

Throwing an Open-Invite, Never-Ending Party with Lilly Pulitzer

Lilly Pulitzer, whose carefree, shoeless Palm Beach lifestyle earned her the moniker "the barefoot tycoon," dreamed up her namesake shift dress while manning a fruit stand on her husband's Florida orange grove in the late 1950s. The frock was vibrantly patterned—to disguise accidental juice spills—and lightweight in the summer heat, complete with a sturdy cotton lining. Soon enough, it became a favorite of chic locals, and eventually, Jackie Kennedy, cementing its place as an easy, breezy American sensation.

In 2015, when Lilly fever was at an all-time high, we partnered with the late designer's brand on a monumental, 250-piece collection. Ironically, although Lilly was known as the ultimate hostess, her line had never included home goods—until the Target collaboration. Everything in the expansive collection served up dreamy visions of Palm Beach: umbrellas in splashy pinks and greens, gold-accented espadrilles, and billowy frocks that embodied a decidedly out-of-office state of mind.

Pulitzer's Target range was so coveted it sold out online and in stores within a few hours; the designer's own daughter, Liza, bemusedly confided to a local newspaper that even she had missed out on the beach chairs she'd been eyeing. On announcing the partnership, a specially created Instagram handle @LillyForTarget was created—within a day, there were 56,000 followers. And in hours of the collection launching, the hashtag #PinkSunday emerged on social media, started by Pulitzer fans. Despite the frenzied clamor from collectors, the boldly patterned pieces still exude a sense of calm: they feel like a South Florida vacation or a party somewhere far-off and sunny, with no need for a plane ticket.

Women wearing Lilly Puiltzer, Palm Beach, photographed by Slim Aarons, 1964

Opposite: Lilly Pulitzer pops her head through a flower made of sheets, photographed by Slim Aarons, 1968

The Making of the Party

Open invite: The Lilly Pulitzer for Target TV commercial was a confetti-covered affair—complete with baby ducks,a giraffe and live flamingo, plus cameos from celebrities of all stripes, including Bella Thorne, Chris Noth and basketballer Nick Young. Pulitzer was a Palm Beach legend, known for larger-than-life parties centered around her home's L-shaped pool. Everyone was invited: from local town fixtures to foreign dignitaries visiting from afar.

To find a set for the summery bash, we searched across the country for a house that looked like a Palm Beach mansion—we found it, in suburban Los Angeles. The pool was only three feet deep, so in the final film scene, when the girl dived into the pool, we worked with a contortionist who could twist in shallow water without hitting the bottom.

Lilly Pulitzer®
Lilly Pulitzer®

Target's line went live online around 3 a.m. I pulled an all-nighter. I was logged in on my computer, iPad and iPhone, along with a group of friends. We kept texting each other with the current status.

In Conversation with Superfan Mary Lane

Interview Laura Bannister
Photography Barbara Anastacio

The Beatles had superfans: throngs of screaming, hyperventilating admirers who knew every lyric by heart, their bedroom walls plastered with posters. Fashion designers have superfans, too—though the most obsessive often play a different role. They're collectors, amateur archivists, and self-taught brand historians. They love how fashion makes them feel.

Mary Lane—an educator and resident of Longwood, Florida—is likely the late Lilly Pulitzer's biggest superfan. She wears the euphoric, summery label every day, has had prints custom-designed after her, and visits her local store weekly, often helping staff unpack new styles. She's loaned garments from her thousands-strong personal collection to museums. She owns two of the brand's most elusive collaborations: a Jeep Wrangler, adorned in a prismatic mash of florals and butterflies, and a jaunty, blushing golf cart. Lane's dog is named Lilly. She's even printed business cards that proclaim herself a brand ambassador. Unsurprisingly, when the Lilly for Target line launched, she pulled an all-nighter to shop it.

LB I'm interested in your earliest memories of Lilly Pulitzer.
ML I grew up playing tennis and loved the Lilly tennis dresses; I'd ride my bike to the courts every day after school and on weekends. In the mid-90s, I remember walking into a Saks Fifth Avenue store in Orlando and there it was: Lilly Pulitzer was back! I was once again in love.

Opposite: Superfan Mary Lane takes a break poolside with her Lilly Pulitzer for Target setup

LB What were some of the first pieces you bought?
ML In the 90s, the line was limited to shift dresses, sweaters, capri pants, and resort wear. It was so preppy. You couldn't make it your complete wardrobe, but it was fun to wear and a real conversation starter. I bought all of the shift dresses I could find, Capri pants, too. Back then, online shopping didn't exist. I made friends with boutiques that carried the line so they'd let me know when new merchandise arrived.

LB Tell me about your rarest items.
ML I have a Lilly Pulitzer street-legal golf cart. There were only a few produced for the Lilly Jubilee in 2010. It's probably the Lilly item I use the most. I live on a golf course, but don't play golf. However, it's the perfect way to get around the neighborhood in style. My dog, Lilly, thinks it's her golf cart—I'm just the chauffeur … Recently, one of the print designers, who is a dear friend, texted me to ask if I'd purchased any [new] items and to look closely because I'd provided some inspiration. There it was, my golf cart with my puppy Lilly comfortably seated in it. What a thrill! I also have some vintage dresses, a vintage tennis ball, a Lilly palm tree made out of Lilly fabric, a golf bag, and some very unique paintings. Most of these were gifts … A bedroom in my house was hand-painted by one of the Lilly artists, too. It features my dog and so many things that are personal to me. It's so fabulous, and it screams Mary Lane.

Too much is never enoug

LB How do friends and family feel about your long-term devotion?
ML It's my signature style. Everywhere I go, people will comment on my outfit. Strangers even stop me and ask, "Is that a Lilly?" At this point in my life, it's hard to separate me from the brand. Lilly doesn't do black very often, and the last time I wore it, everyone thought someone had died.

LB A lot of brands have superfans. What draws people to this one?
ML The print is exceptional in that it can be anything: turtles, lobsters, sailboats, even an occasional streaker. The print team goes on inspirational trips—all the fun they have gets translated into prints. It's like going on a virtual vacation. Not many other brands design their own prints to the same extent—for instance, did you know that in every Lilly print you will find the word Lilly? [Finding it] makes for great fun in boring meetings.

LB What's one piece of Lilly trivia that no one—bar a superfan—would know?
ML There are several, but I don't want to spill all the family secrets. Her swimming pool was in the shape of an "L." The "L" on her front door was duplicated on some of the first stores. She always had a pitcher of iced tea in her refrigerator and would drape leaves from tropical plants over the top so that when poured, there was an essence of the tropics. Her home was a lush jungle. She had cats and dogs that roamed freely. On one visit, she was raising baby rats in a box because she wanted to make sure they had a fighting chance before she turned them loose.

LB You knew Lilly personally. How did your friendship begin?
ML The third corporate store that was opened was in Winter Park, Florida, and it's still my home away from home. I remember the excitement when I saw the wood façade on Park Avenue announcing Lilly Pulitzer was coming soon. I would walk by and peek in with anticipation. Finally, I got a sneak peek before it opened and then was one of the first ones, if not the first, to walk in the door the day it opened. Lilly hadn't been in one of her stores since she closed her business in the 80s. The store manager invited me to have lunch with Lilly there. I remember the look on Lilly's face when she stepped through the door. It was utter amazement! For the longest time, she walked through the store asking, "Is that a Lilly?" She was like a proud mom seeing the rebirth of her brand. We spent the afternoon together, chatted and laughed a lot. She recognized my love for the brand and said I needed to visit her when I was in Palm Beach. Palm Beach is small—she'd find out if you were in town and didn't stop by. I began to visit her there and we became special friends.

LB Is it true you threw the designer her 80th birthday party?
ML Yes! The Museum of Lifestyle and Fashion History in Palm Beach County had a vintage Lilly exhibit. With Lilly's upcoming 80th birthday, they decided to hold a party. I was the host and chair of the event. It was a labor of love doing it long distance, with help from Lisa Stuart in Key West and Barbara Malone in Connecticut. Lilly really did not want to have a party. She didn't know what all the fuss was about, so she went kicking and screaming. Once she got there and saw all the Lilly décor—and over 100 guests who had traveled from across the US to celebrate with her, she was thrilled.

Opposite: Mary Lane in her Lilly Pulitzer-themed bedroom

LB The collaboration with Target sold out impossibly fast, with near-immediate eBay markups. You flew to NYC for the launch. What was so important about being in New York for it?
ML The Bryant Park launch took place a few days before the Lilly for Target line was available. There was so much excitement surrounding the collaboration and I wanted to experience it. The evening before the launch in the park, they hosted a private party. They had a small shop set up with the Target line and you could purchase five items. Luckily, I went to the checkout line where the person checking you out couldn't count very well! My friend Heather joined me in NYC. I remember waking up several times during the night and looking out on the park to see if a line was forming. At about 6 a.m., several people were already in line, so we hurried down to join the fun.

The event opened up to the public the following day—what a party it was! The fountain was dyed pink, and everywhere you looked there were Lilly umbrellas, hammocks, beach chairs, ping pong tables—even live painting by Lilly print artists. Target's line went live online around 3 a.m..

I pulled an all-nighter. I was logged in on my computer, iPad, and iPhone along with a group of friends. We kept texting each other with the current status. At 6 a.m., we'd done all the damage we could so we went to the largest Target store in the area.The line was immense. We'd scoped out the store and had a game plan. We divided up and hit the ground running—literally—when the doors opened. In less than ten minutes, the store was completely sold out.

LB What do you think Lilly would have made of the partnership?
ML I think she would have loved the collaboration. Lilly grew up in a wealthy environment but she wasn't snobbish in any way. She loved life and seized every opportunity to have fun. I think she would have been delighted with the idea that so many people wanted to purchase these items.

LB For a lot of people, an interest in fashion can be seen as frivolous. But fashion is connected to everything: art, politics, culture, the way we express ourselves to the world. What does it mean to you?
ML For me, wearing Lilly is a way to express yourself without saying a word. Two people can wear the same piece and style it completely differently. I often choose based on my mood or agenda for the day. The staff at the Lilly stores have become friends. They know how excited I get when a new delivery arrives, so I'm usually right there before it even hits the floor. One of my best Lilly friends is Heather—we met in line at the Lilly warehouse sale many years ago. She lives in the Philadelphia area but we talk almost daily. We try to get together at least once a year; we call it Camp Lilly. This past summer we met up and were joined by Trish, another dear friend. Trish showed up with totes monogrammed "Camp Lilly."

LB That's incredible. I do wonder—how far have you gone to track down a piece?
ML I will go to ends of the earth to find a Lilly piece that I "need." Whether this means flying to NYC for the Target launch or searching eBay for the one that got away. Lilly's legacy lives on in a brand that's survived 60 years and counting. For an American brand, that's amazing.

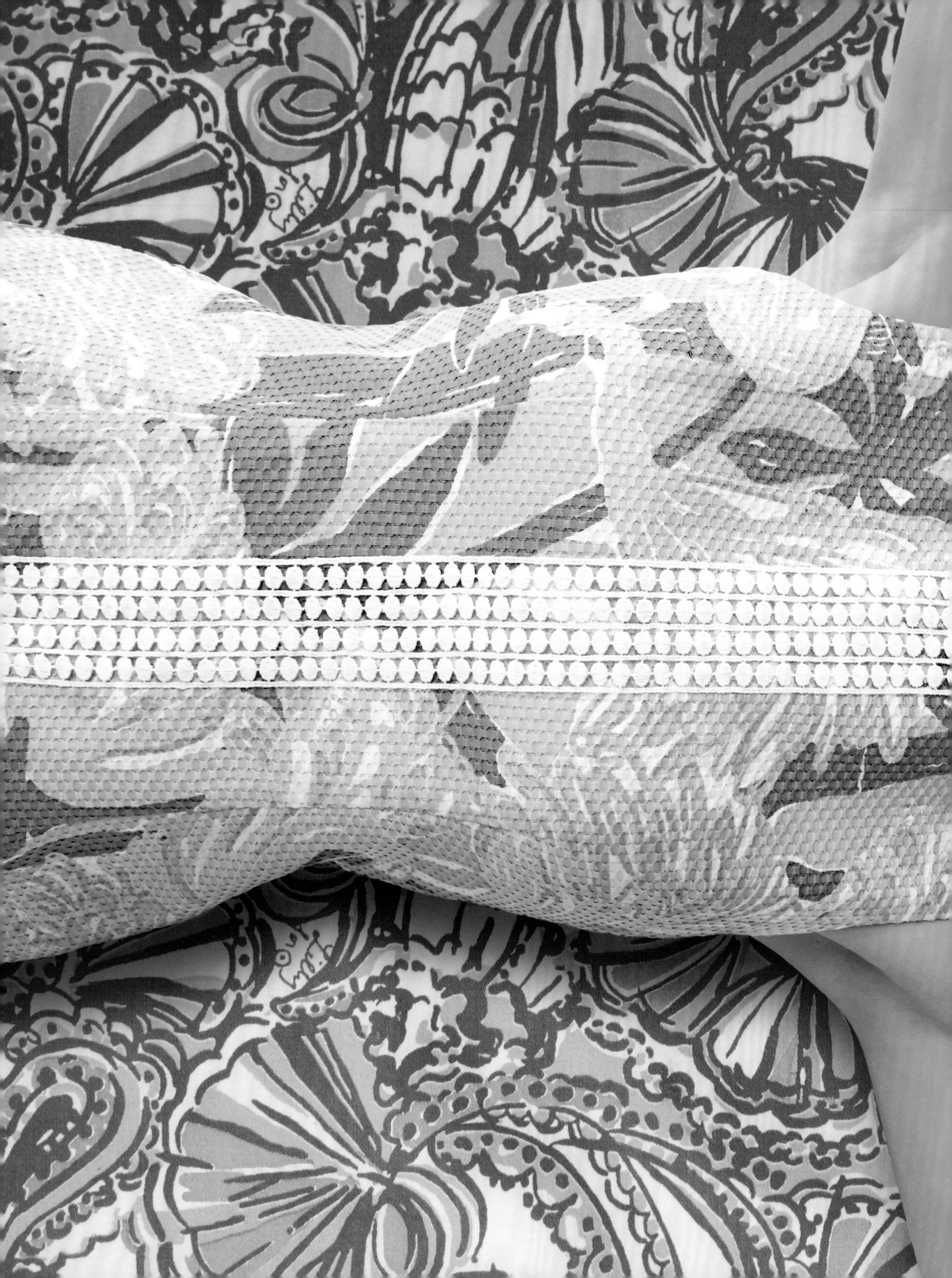

In Pulitzer's eyes, life was a party, and celebrations didn't require a special occasion.

Lilly Pulitzer

Lilly Pulitzer products sold out so fast there were reports of people asking if they could take the store signs home.

Marimekko

2016

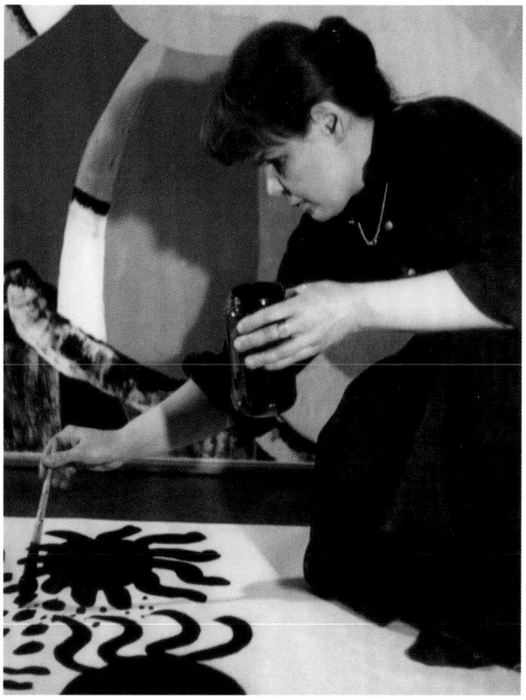

Together with Marimekko, We Brought Finnish Summers to the States

Is there a secret sauce behind iconic prints? Established in the 1950s, Marimekko was at the forefront of a wave of Scandinavian designers who had a lasting influence on the way we see the world, from textiles to products to architecture. Married founders Armi and Viljo Ratia were committed to working with artists to transform functional household objects and apparel into magical color-soaked sources of inspiration. They worked closely with a suite of brilliant minds to craft memorable, graphic motifs—jaunty, joyful shapes that seemed to mimic fruit and modernist, abstract florals—and printed them on repeat across everything: boxy dresses, button-downs, sturdy tablecloths. (Also radical: at a time when design was dominated by men, Marimekko stood out for its support of working women. At one point its workforce was over 90% female.) Often, the brand's duplicated shapes are inspired by fresh, clean forms found in Mother Nature—which is perhaps what makes them so enduring. In our 200-plus piece-collaboration with the famous Finns, there were several design firsts—including a play parachute. Every print was dreamt up by Marimekko designer Maija Isola.

Designer Maija Isola, photographed by Asko Tolonen/ Designmuseum, Helsinki

Opposite: Archival Marimekko photographed by Tony Vaccaro for *Life*, 1965

Style is Served

Prints resembling oranges, perfectly sliced, and dyed the summery hues of sunshine and sky. A wavy form moving across plates and trays in ultramarine, the exact color prized by Renaissance painters. Our Marimekko tableware abounded with floral prints, fruit, and crisp whites set against watery blues. It was perfect for ad-hoc layering or on its own as a feature. Whatever really—in summer, you make your own rules.

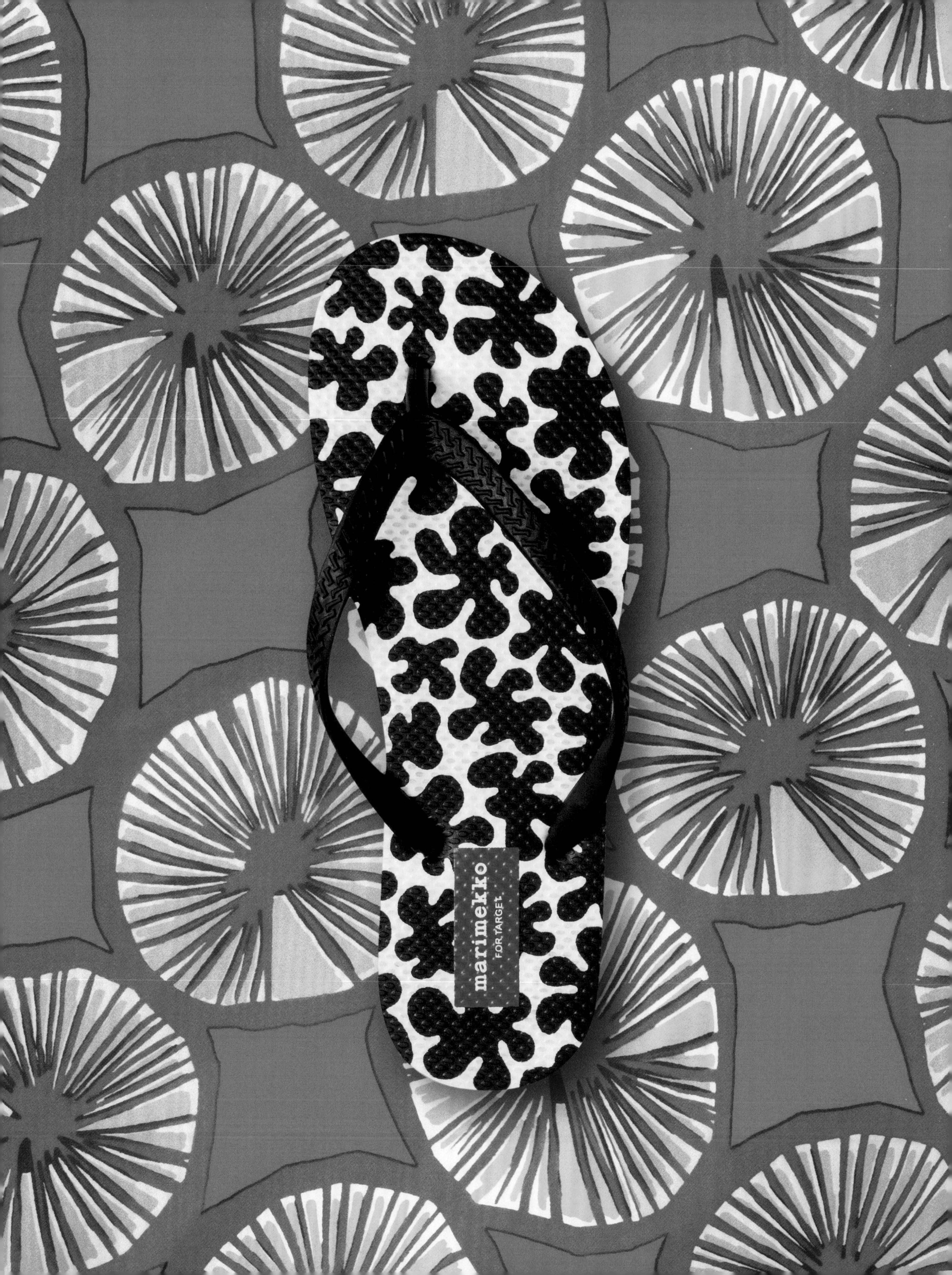
marimekko
FOR TARGET

En Plein Air: When Marimekko Owned the Sky

Built on a former elevated railroad line, New York's High Line officially opened in 2009. It's the only park in the city featuring an art program curated around its unique topography, with the goal of fusing sky-high art and ordinary life. While the High Line is a successor to a series of public art projects (think the lifelong work of artists Christo and Jean-Claude, who've wrapped everything from Australia's coastline to the Pont Neuf in Paris), it played host to a special guest in 2016: Marimekko for Target. Ahead of the collection's launch in-store, we took over the High Line with joyful, organic-seeming forms, each splashed with Finnish prints. The giant soft sculptures oozed out of entryways for the public to touch and play on, forming pop-up bounce houses for kids. Art is all around us, as Marimekko knows—and it's more inviting than we think.

Marimekko for Target installation at the High Line, photographed by Evan Savitt

Lennätä Leijaa,
TargetStyle.

Go Fly A Kite,
TargetStyle.

Surffaamaan,
TargetStyle.

Surf's Up,
TargetStyle.

Finnish, TargetStyle.

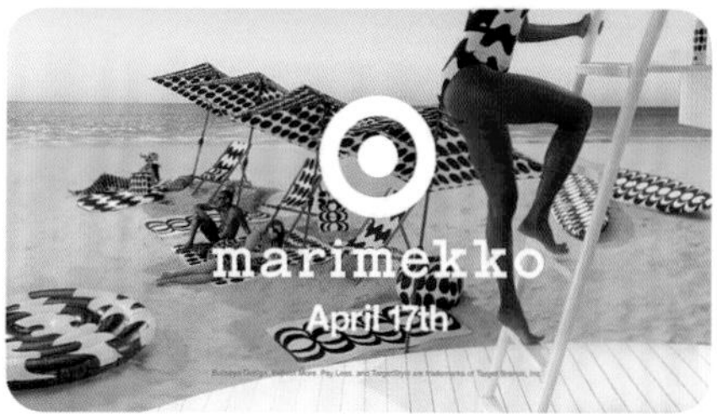
marimekko
April 17th

Hei, Hello. As a tribute to the remarkable—and Helsinki-headquartered brand—all the text in our Marimekko TV commercial appeared in Finnish first and was later translated to English. 89% of Finland's population speak their native tongue.

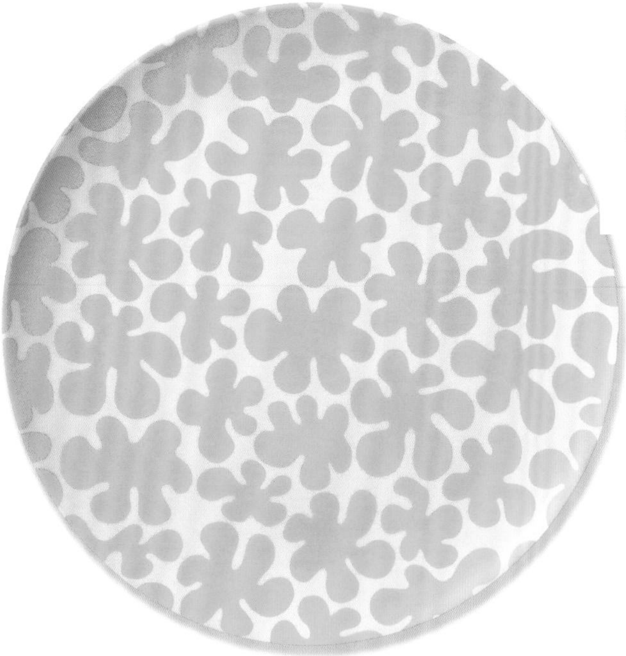

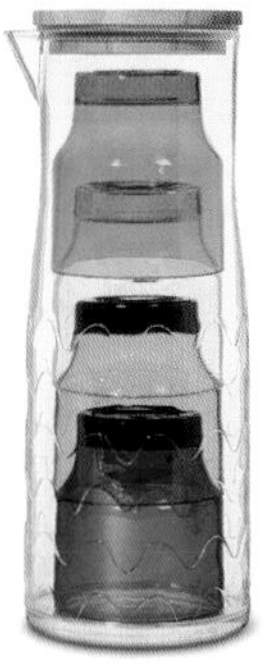

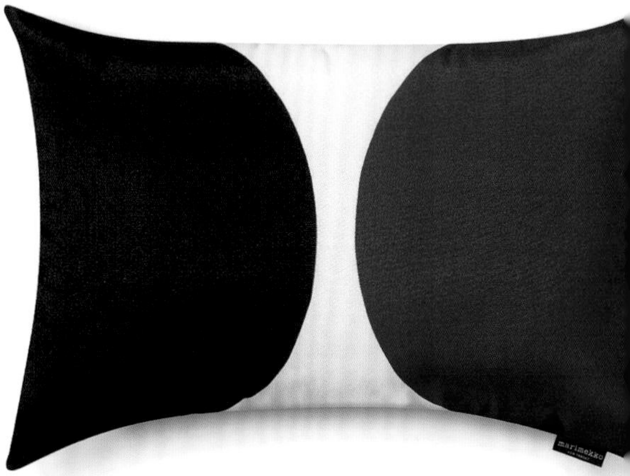

The collection was inspired by Finnish summers, where the sunlight hours stretch out 'til midnight.

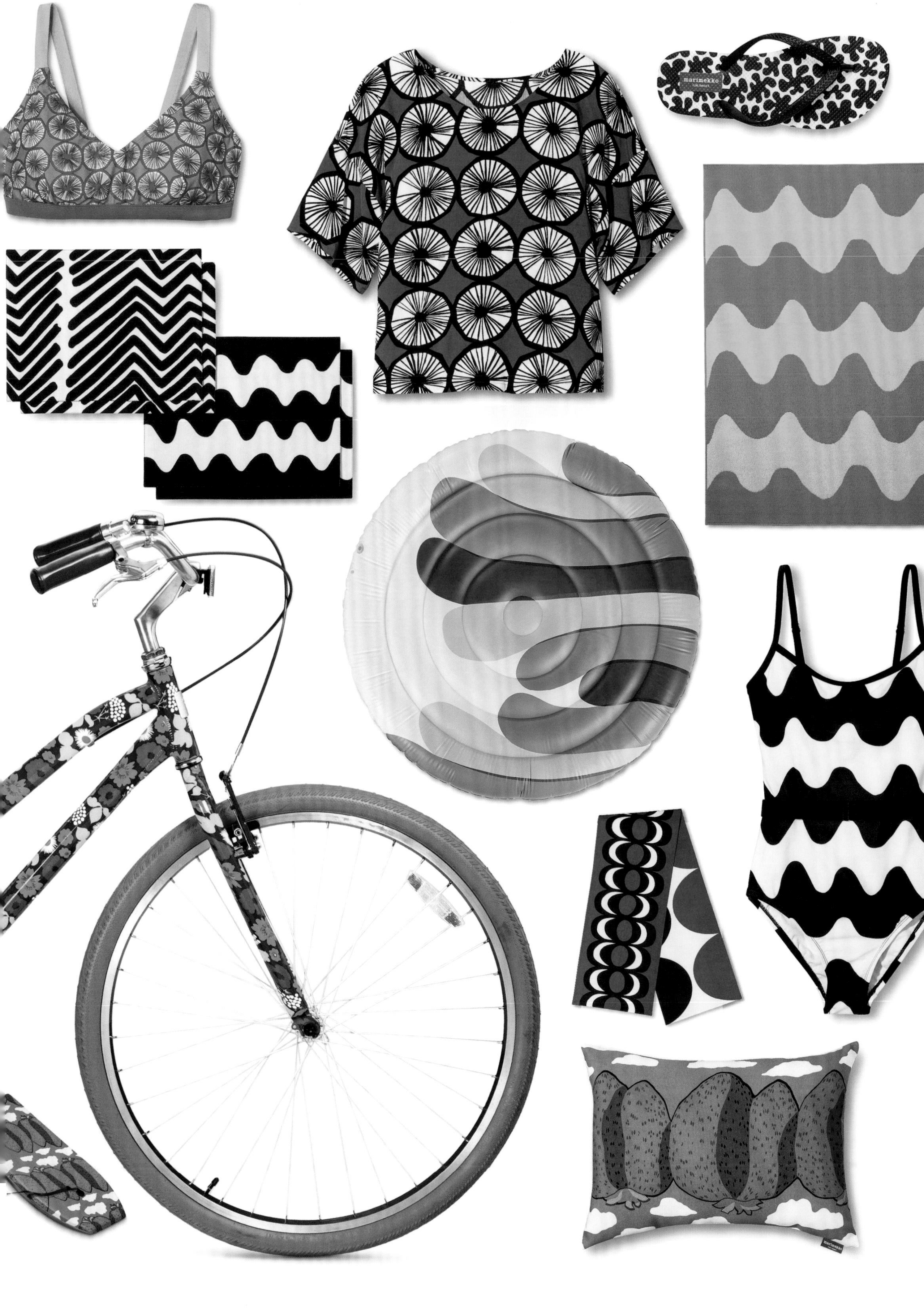

Peter
Pilotto
2014

Prints Charming: Inside Peter Pilotto's Hi-Tech Digital Universe

In 2018, the British duo behind Peter Pilotto—Pilotto himself and fellow creative director Christopher de Vos—catapulted to a level of fashion fame near-impossible to top. On a blustery fall day, Princess Eugenie revealed her wedding-day gown to a crowd of royal guests: a custom Peter Pilotto. It was long-sleeved and white and made from silk jacquard; the neckline folded just so. From the masters of layered, kaleidoscopic color, it was unusual—but Peter Pilotto has always been a master of surprise.

More than a decade before receiving its royal seal of approval, the brand was still beloved by London's coolest. Its hyper-layered prints were created digitally—then embellished with beading—which often tricked the wearer into seeing visual vibrations.

Putting on a Pilotto dress was like slipping into a *Magic Eye* book. In 2014, at the height of Pilotto obsession, we tapped the designers to work on a 60-piece summer collection—all form-fitting architectural dresses, punchy sneakers and jewel-toned, mosaic totes.

The phenomenal partnership was full of firsts: the British label had never before made accessories, and select items were stocked on luxury retailer Net-a-Porter, marking Target's debut on the site. This enabled international high fashion fans to shop our partnerships for the first time. According to *British Vogue*, it was Net-a-Porter's highest selling launch to date, with orders "placed every second for an hour" on launch day—a right royal result.

Opposite:
Peter Pilotto and Christopher de Vos, photographed by Kate Marin, 2014

Since the duo is known for their manipulation of print and pattern, what better way to highlight the presentation—in this beautifully historic space—than an elaborate center-piece of mirrors and video, constantly changing perspectives of the collection from every vantage point.

Scott Swartz, VP Creative, Target

Peter Pilotto for Target launch, photographed by Jamie McGregor Smith

Opposite: Campaign featuring Jourdan Dunn, photographed by Craig McDean

Pilotto and de Vos update traditional couture by digitally designing patterns, creating otherworldly colors that are both sharp and deep.

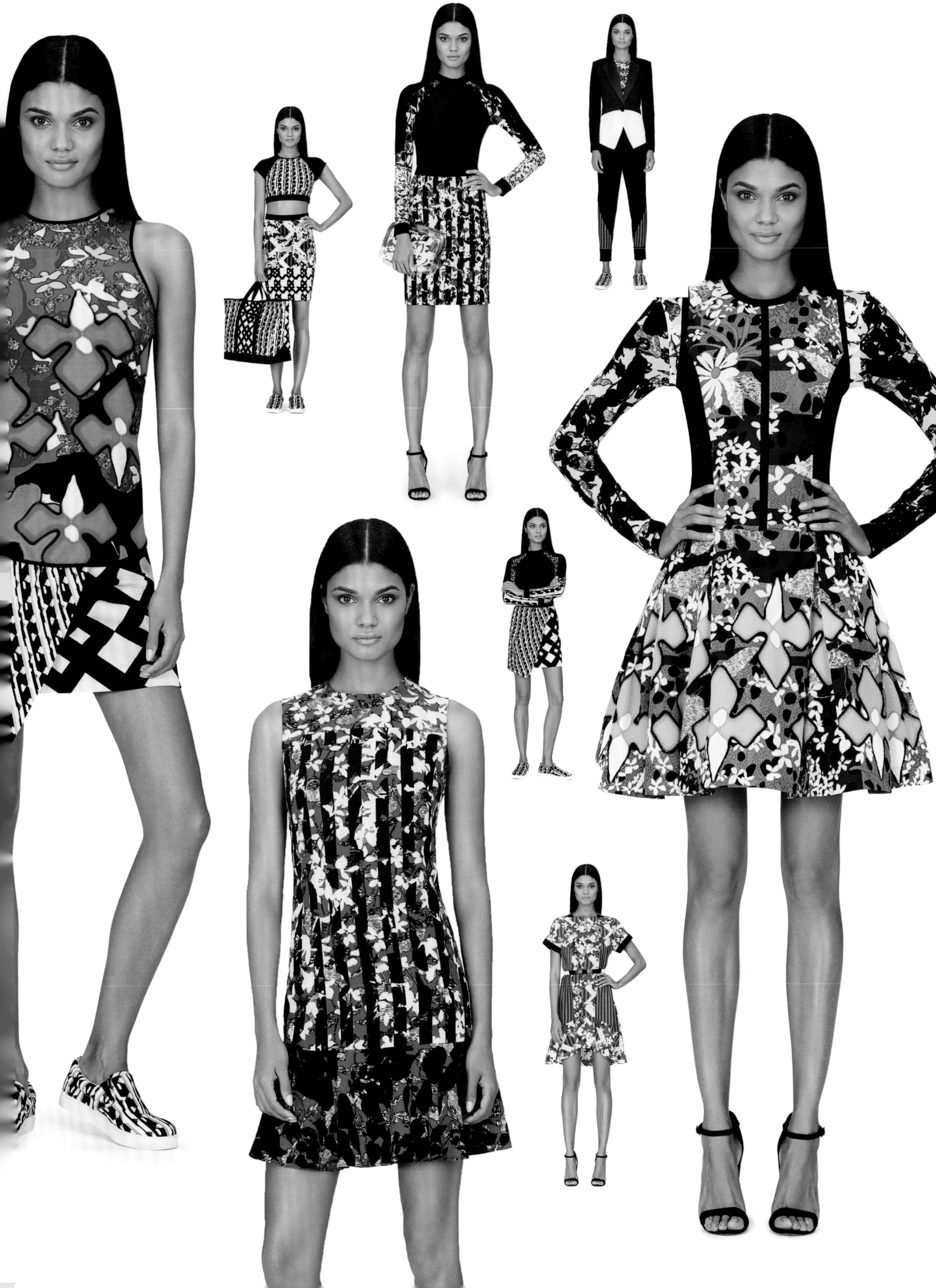

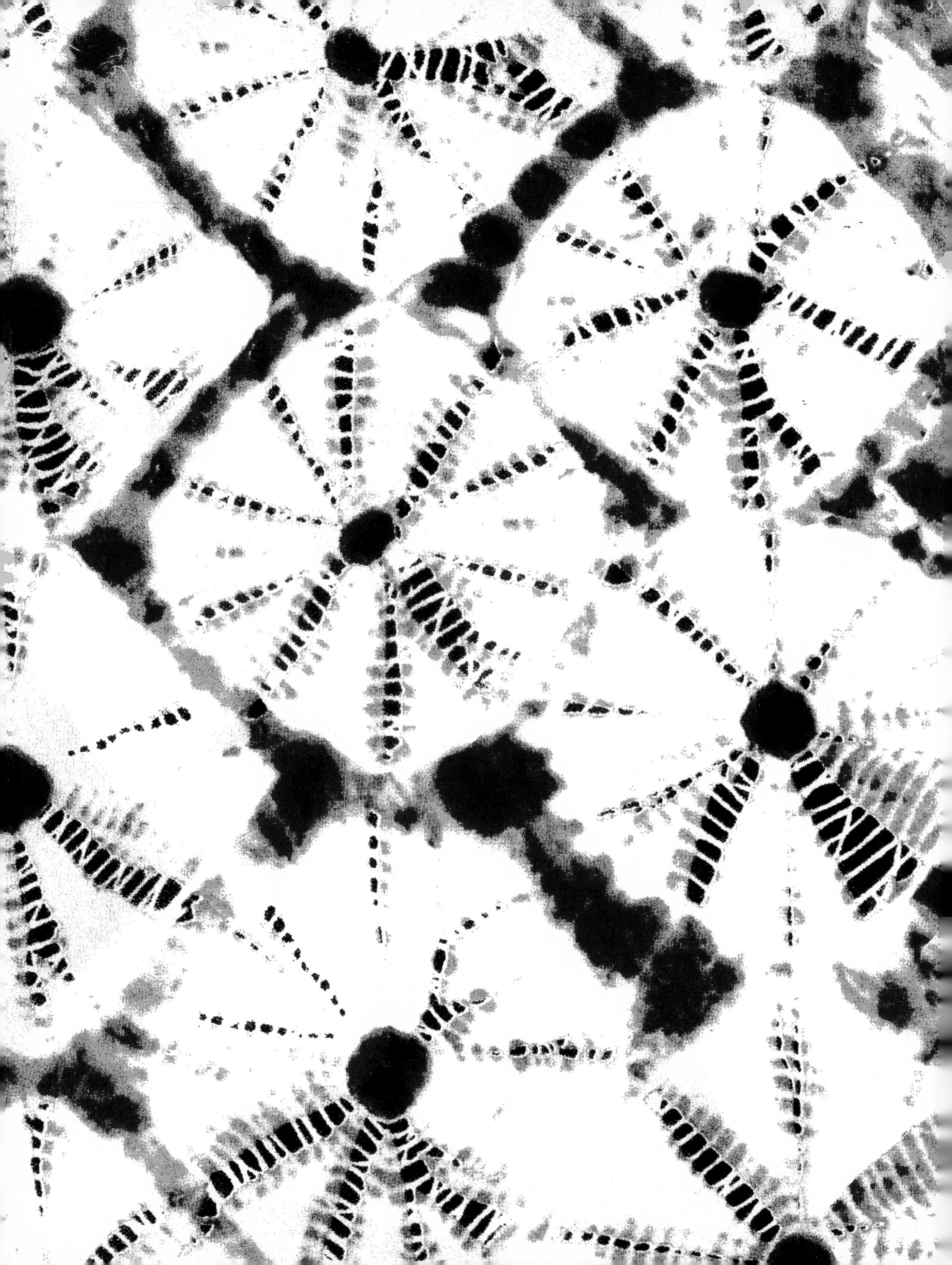

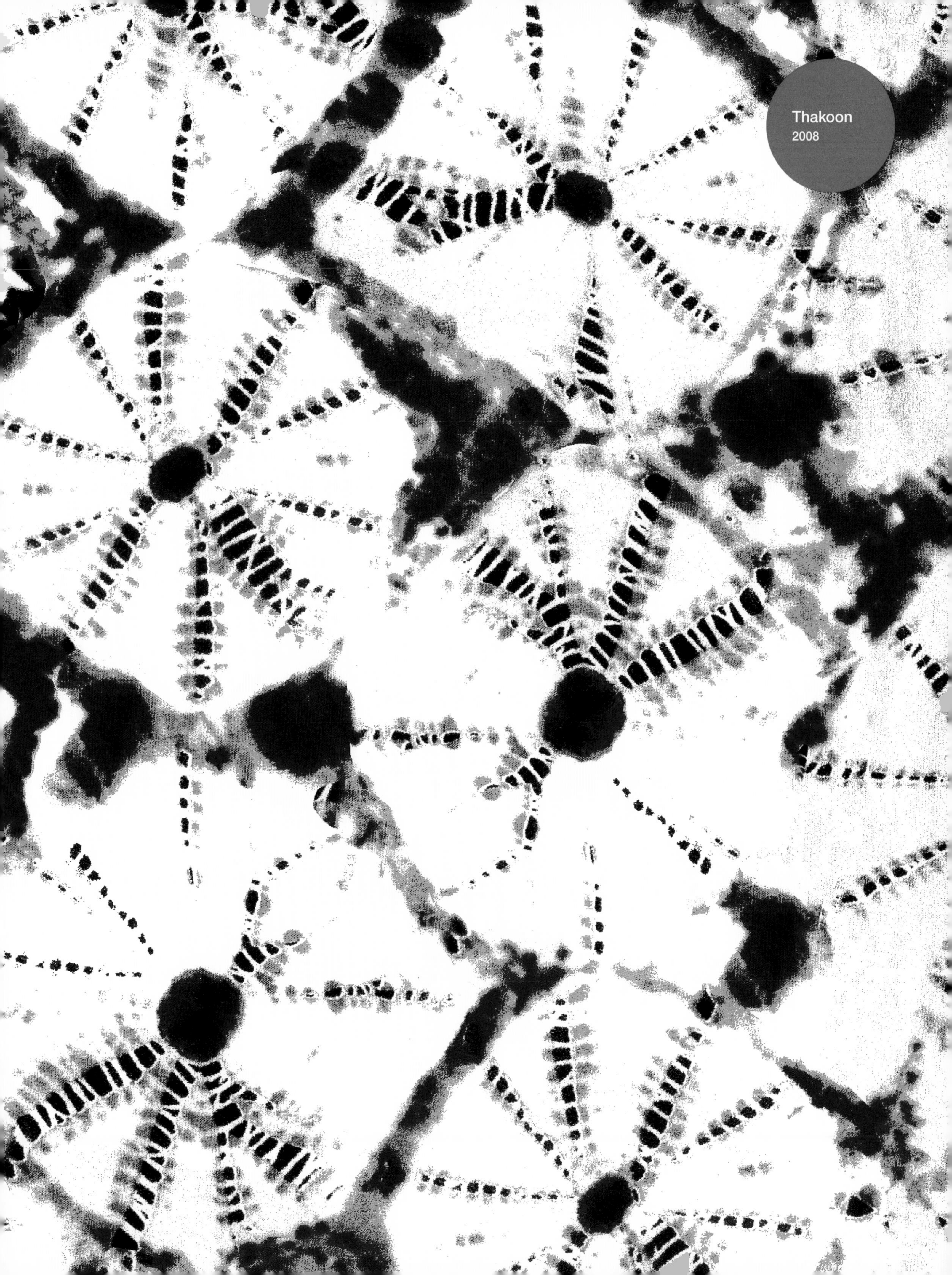

Thakoon
2008

We Went Full Bloom with the Artful Eye of Thakoon

At age 11, Thakoon Panichgul moved with his family from Bangkok to Omaha, Nebraska—and quickly found himself enamored by fashion magazines. Growing up, the Thai designer's eye was instantly drawn to images of classic Americana: the perfect simplicity of a white button-down shirt, the ease of blue jeans. It was an allure that would eventually emerge in what the *New York Times* dubbed an effortless and "distinctly American aesthetic."

In 2004, after leaving his job as a writer at *Harper's Bazaar* to debut his own line, Thakoon was thrust into the public eye. His flower-forward, uniquely feminine dresses had gained a loyal fan base among celebrities like Sarah Jessica Parker and Julianne Moore. It wasn't until four years later—when then-First Lady Michelle Obama appeared on stage at the Democratic National Convention in a puff-sleeved Thakoon number—that the designer became a household name. In late December that same year, with Thakoon still in a post-Obama glow, we snatched him up to launch a collaborative line, offering holiday cheer in the form of dark, tropical florals, prismatic purples, clean greens and Japanese Shibori-inspired prints. It was easy elegance, the big city meets the tropics—just as Thakoon likes it.

Thakoon Panichgul, photographed by Evan Sung

Opposite: Michelle Obama wears a Thakoon dress at the Democratic National Convention, photographed by Joe Raedle, 2008

My mom loved the picture of Mrs. Obama in Thakoon at the Democratic National Convention. So she was thrilled to find something of Mrs. Obama's style at an affordable price. It's great to show affordable fashion is not just for the young.

Mary Hall, Thakoon fan

This page and opposite: Campaign photographed by Horst Diekgerdes

Prabal
Gurung
2013

Cinematic Attraction: On Falling in Love with Prabal Gurung

On catching a glimpse of American-Nepalese fashion designer Prabal Gurung's pieces, people sit up a little straighter—they pay attention. The suits are dangerously sharp, the dresses all defiant neons, bisected florals and cutouts at the sides. More recently, the cashmere is dip-dyed. Gurung's clothes are notorious for making bold statements, and they have been since the designer captured fashion imaginations nearly two decades ago with his eponymous label. A perfectionist—to put it lightly—the designer's obsession with detail took the idea of ready-to-wear luxury to a new level, one that intrigued the likes of Kate Middleton and Michelle Obama.

With the world's gaze, Gurung rooted his fashion in raising a greater awareness of global needs, including starting a foundation to help underprivileged children in his homeland of Nepal.

In 2013, we teamed up with Gurung, just days before Valentine's Day, to release a nearly 90-plus piece collection inspired by the different stages of love, wherever in the world the wearer might be. We indulged, exchanging bouquets for head-turning blazers, and trading heart-shaped chocolates for tempting pendant necklaces. As always, Gurung caught everyone's attention: the line nearly sold out in a day.

Prabal Gurung, courtesy Spring Studios

Opposite:
From the Prabal Gurung campaign film, *Love*, featuring Olivia Thirlby, photographed by Darius Khondji

This page and opposite: Prabal Gurung for Target launch event, photographed by Susie Montagna for David Stark Design & Production –

Prabal's collection reflected the many stages of love, so the February launch was the ultimate first date experience: an elaborate carnival held on Pier 57. As Scott Swartz, VP Creative at Target recalls: "From food, to rides, to a performance by Ne-Yo, everyone fell in love with the collection. It was one of the more memorable ways we've launched a collaboration, right before Fashion Week."

Gurung's bright prints are inspired by Bollywood, which he explored while at the National Institute of Fashion Technology, New Delhi.

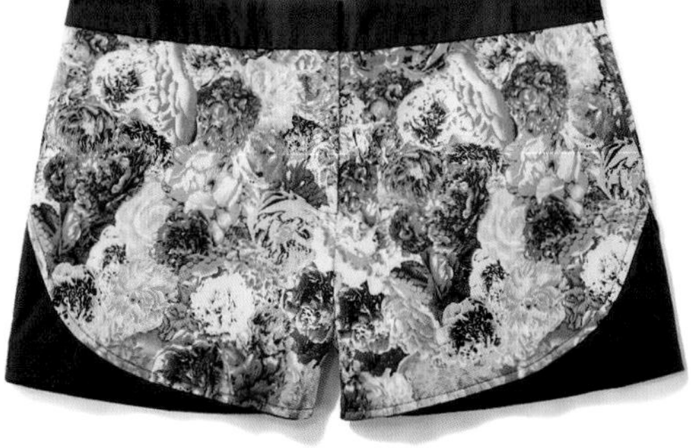

Opposite:
The Prabal Gurung for Target TV commercial filming was interrupted by Hurricane Sandy, which brought NYC to a standstill.

They never let reality interfere with flights of fancy. Be it a traditional garden hose made hot pink, pastel roller skates, or melamine trays where butterfly wings perched on collaged paper, each of these optimists reinvented everyday objects with playfulness and humor. Often, their wares are made for entertaining—think dinner sets and unexpected party pleasers. Case in point: the line of towering foam Halloween wigs by *Project Runway* alum Chris March—deliriously campy bouffants opening portals to worlds of fun—or just about anything by Cynthia Rowley.

Todd Oldham
2002–

Sonia Kashuk
1999–

Cynthia Rowley
2003+2008

Marcus Samuelsson
2010

Isabel and Ruben Toledo
2010

Museum of Ice Cream
2018

Askov Finlayson
2018

John Derian
2008+2010

Oh Joy!
2014-2017

Harajuku Mini
2011-2012

Chris March
2013+2014

Luella Bartley
2006

Optimists

Todd Oldham
2002—

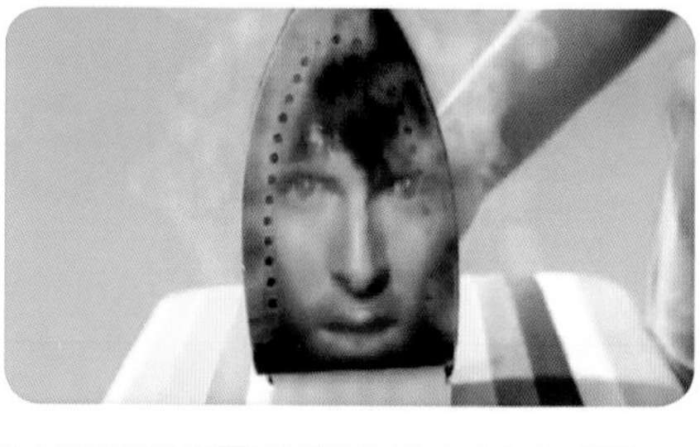

Cut and Paste: How Todd Oldham's Craft Skills Changed Fashion

Poster paints, pipe cleaners and food dye—oh my! Designer Todd Oldham brought the craft of fashion to the small screen in the 90s with his regular "Todd Time" segment on MTV's *House of Style*. Introduced by supermodel host Cindy Crawford each week, these three-minute DIY sessions saw Oldham educate a generation of runway obsessives on how to hand-make their own custom couture. Using little more than art-store supplies, thrift shop finds and hot glue, Oldham crafted his way into the American living room with his delightful mix of high fashion credentials and dollar store materials. In keeping with the 90s cut-and-paste aesthetic, he helped democratize fashion into something anyone could participate in.

Bright, bold and bursting with color, "Todd Time" mirrored the energy of Oldham's runways as he shared his most practical tips and tricks plucked from his time in the fashion trade for just a few thrilling moments a week. Beloved by the viewing public (and a natural-born entertainer), Oldham would go on to host *Fashionably Loud* on MTV, be a mentor on Bravo's *Top Design* and present his own show *Handmade Modern*, joined by a motley crew of collaborators—including comedian Amy Sedaris and actors Susan Sarandon and Elizabeth Berkley—for an assortment of adventures in design.

Oldham moved to New York in 1989, an 18-year-old from Texas with pink hair and a penchant for roller skating. He grew up transforming thrifted clothes into new creations in his family garage, and quickly turned his sharp craft skills into a major fashion line. His clothes were embraced by models, club kids, and celebrities, who often walked in his shows: RuPaul, Rosie O'Donnell, and Christian Slater all strutted down runways in his complex, colorful get-ups.

"Fashion is very noisy, and it kind of sticks with people in funny ways, considering it's this ephemeral thing we often just toss under the bed or in the dryer," he told the *New York Times*. The nonstop grind of the fashion show cycle began to wear on Oldham, and in 1997, after years of critical and financial success, he retired his namesake brand, trying his hand at editorials, among other things. In 2002, he debuted a new collaboration with us called Todd Oldham Home, a collection of back-to-school wares (including bedding, backpacks, and more) that he described as "varsity funk, a little punky, a little preppy."

A decade later, he introduced Kids Made Modern, an ongoing collection of arts and crafts materials and DIY kits. Skip three years and he followed it up with Hand Made Modern, a similar line aimed at adults. He called it a "celebration of my love of making stuff," adding, "Arts and crafts has been a big part of my life and good quality materials are the essence of being able to have success." It's the latest chapter in a life he's spent helping people create beautiful things at home.

Todd Oldham, photographed by Catherine McGann, 1992

Opposite: Stills from Todd Oldham for Target TV commercial

EXIT C
KID MADE MODERN
THANK YOU TO OUR PARTNERS

I love From Carlet
ToDD OlDham

Target and Todd Oldham team up to make over a Staten Island school library

Crafts for a Cause: Todd Oldham's Library Renovation

In 2012, Todd Oldham teamed up with us to renovate a Staten Island elementary school. Oldham's lifelong interest in craft carried over to the Kids Made Modern and Hand Made Modern lines he designed for us, and his decades of experience made him the perfect choice to lead the renovation of the library and art room at P.S. 21 Margaret Emery-Elm Park—still recovering in the wake of Hurricane Sandy. We contributed brand new furniture, carpet, shelving, technology upgrades, and Kid Made Modern art supplies, transforming the rooms into inviting, nurturing spaces, ready for mini bookworms. We donated 2,000 books to fill the library shelves, as part of our Target School Library Makeover program, which has renovated over 200 libraries across America, and donated more than 1.5 million books.

"I loved hanging out in the library when I was a kid; it was a never-ending surprise," said Oldham. "The library ignited my lifelong love of reading and books." In thinking about how to make the space more inviting, he opted for tones that felt at once warm and vibrant, in order to establish "a sunny and optimistic arena to learn and create."

Oldham has dedicated his career to making craft and design accessible. It's not just about the aesthetics—he believes deeply in democratizing the tools needed to create beauty, and we're glad to have played a small part in it.

Sonia
Kashuk
1999–

The Making of Sonia Kashuk's "Mass-tige" Makeup Movement

Sonia Kashuk has been referred to as the First Lady of Designer Makeup. Her career began with a surprising lucky break—after attending art school in Minneapolis, where she grew up, a friend asked her to fill in on the set of a music video shoot; the makeup artist had canceled last minute. The song was "Funkytown" by Lipps Inc, which went on to become one of the biggest hits of the 80s. Excited, Kashuk transferred to beauty school, and before long she caught the attention of the legendary photographer Arthur Elgort. She moved to New York City, where he introduced her to the editors at *Vogue*, who she worked with for more than 15 years. Kashuk's best friend—Cindy Crawford—also moved to NYC around that time. In 1997, the pair collaborated on a book titled *Cindy Crawford's Basic Face*.

Growing up middle-class in the Midwest, Kashuk had always wanted to transform makeup into something accessible to women like her and her sisters. At the time, the tools and techniques used by professionals were prohibitively expensive. So Kashuk connected with us (we'd learned of her work from the Crawford book), and in 1999, we partnered on a line of affordable cosmetics. Kashuk called the concept "mass-tige": prestige looks aimed at a wider audience. It was a perfect match with our "Design for All" philosophy, and cemented her as the first ever makeup artist to partner with a major retailer. She was overjoyed with the collection, telling *Forbes*, "Women everywhere could afford to have the best in beauty."

Sonia Kashuk, photographed by Richard Burbridge

Opposite: A selection of items from Sonia Kashuk for Target collection

by cynthia rowley

Swell™

and ilene rosenzweig

Cynthia
Rowley
2003+2008

A charming two-tone bug towel, antennas and all by Cynthia Rowley for Target

Opposite:
Cynthia Rowley, photographed by LIFE Picture Collection, 1990

In Conversation with Cynthia Rowley

Interview by Laura Bannister

In one of her fashion shows, Cynthia Rowley enlisted a throng of roller derby athletes in place of models. As they glided through her West Village office, the scene was one of jubilant chaos: a flurry of flowery jumpsuits, rubber wheels, and gingham swing dresses. In another presentation, Rowley's models stormed the perimeter of an indoor pool, before the last of them jumped in, splashing while donning pastel wetsuits.

Rowley is not prone to one-off gimmicks—her entire career is imbued with a sense of unpredictability and no-rules fun. (As for the wetsuits, she's an avid surfer too, and has designed prints for a slew of surfboards.) Since launching her first womenswear capsule in the late 80s, the Illinois-born, New York-based designer has tried her hand at everything: fragrances, swimwear, home furnishings, cosmetics and office accessories—many of them debuting in our stores. Inspired by her own love of entertaining, Rowley's 2003 Swell for Target line included rainbow ice buckets and trays for cocktail hour (and later, extended from housewares to activewear, intimates and sleepwear), while her 2008 Whim collection was all outdoorsy staples in saturated hues: towels, badminton rackets, even baby blue grills.

When I spoke to the designer, she was in her New York studio: an old mechanic's garage with plenty of space for big projects. She still remembers her work with Target: "When I started and was so small, I spent so many years hearing everyone say no. So to have the giant support of Target saying yes to bringing beauty to everyday necessities—it was a dream come true."

LAURA BANNISTER How did your collaborations with Target begin?
CYNTHIA ROWLEY In 2000, I met someone from the Target team at a cocktail party. He asked if I would ever do something with Target. This was very early on—we were having runway shows and dressing celebrities—I wasn't totally sure if other people would understand the concept of an accessible collection. But it was something I truly believed in and what I thought was the future of great design. I shopped like this—I knew all my friends did too—so the idea of adding value to a product without price, simply by making it look elevated and cool, was ahead of its time. At the same time, my best friend Ilene Rosenzweig and I had just written a bestselling book called *Swell: A Girl's Guide to the Good Life*, filled with entertaining tips and ways to live with *joie de vivre*. This became the perfect manifesto for the Swell lifestyle products. How to disguise take-out food as home-cooked for a dinner party, how to add spark to your post-dorm room décor, and how to transform your PJs into a cute cocktail outfit. We designed 700 products per year for three years and built a $100-million-dollar-a-year business.

Why hadn't anyone made a baby blue Weber grill or a pink garden hose before? I thought maybe you need it—maybe you just can't live without it.

Whim by Cynthia Rowley for Target, campaign photographed by Curtis Johnson

LB You've said that part of your modus operandi is to "go into uncharted territory." What were the never-before-done bits of Swell and Whim?
CR Every product was a new adventure, something I had never designed before. Our MO was to design things that had been completely overlooked—Target supported all of our big ideas. There was a pink garden hose, a baby blue BBQ, striped trash bags, pool floaties, round beach towels (so you only have to turn your body, not your towel), and a disposable camera that won a design award. All this was in addition to the bread and butter [categories]: bed, bath and tabletop.

LB How much freedom were you given on each line? Did it change when you began Whim, and already had a working relationship together?
CR It really felt like the sky was the limit and it was a very collaborative process. We were all excited about bringing in a new customer and transforming the guest experience. When we came back a few years later to do the Whim collection, the product development team was a well-oiled machine. We designed everything on paper and they executed it perfectly. I've always felt that Target was the perfect home for us to launch new ideas, so when we were the first to do designer Band-Aids for Johnson+Johnson, there was only one place to launch them.

LB Did you ever go to the headquarters in Minneapolis, or were you working from your studio in NYC?
CR We were in Minneapolis all the time and, being a Midwest girl at heart, it was always so much fun. We would go for design meetings, campaign meetings, and—before there were Target stores in NYC—we'd fly home with huge bags after a shopping spree at the store. There was a funny time when I forgot to bring my photo ID to use my credit card at checkout, so I just pointed to a giant photo of myself in aisle five. That did the trick!

LB The Whim line abounded with summer staples and novelties: blow-up pieces, croquet sets and floppy hats. How did you approach getting the balance right between fun and functional, or ensure something that was novel still stood up design-wise?
CR So many summer essentials are completely overlooked in design. Why hadn't anyone made a baby blue Weber grill or a pink garden hose before? I thought maybe you need it—maybe you just can't live without it. Ultimately, it was easy because Target makes the best quality products, so if it makes you happy every time you look at it, even better. Summer is my scene, so maybe someday we'll be back to do foam surfboards with matching swimsuits.

LB I remember you made this amazing *Sex and the City*-style TV commercial for the Swell collection; a sort of rapturous, tongue-in-cheek film of a party where anything goes. There were a lot of slapstick moments too. What inspired it?
CR Real life! The Swell for Target collection showed that the good life was not about a paycheck, but rather a state of mind. I'm pretty sure there were real cocktails in those glasses and that toss into the trash bag was a single take. We were so excited to see it air—it debuted during the Golden Globes!

LB How did Target change things for Cynthia Rowley as a brand? What was your post-Target world like?
CR Target changed everything. We wrote three more books translated in many languages and basically became a household name. We did *Oprah*, *Letterman*, *The View*, *The Today Show* … people still ask me where they can find the product. It's only helped my designer collection. The Swell girl has grown up and now goes to our site to find a pretty dress or the perfect swimsuit for her next adventure.

LB I wonder, when you're making collaborative work like this, what the most rewarding part is. Is it seeing the end-product on shelves, or in homes? Is it using it yourself? Or is there some kind of magic that comes when you join forces with someone else and start swapping ideas?
CR I always say the best part of my job is having an idea and being able to make it a reality. I found that working with Target gave me the opportunity to tell a story. My daughter just moved into her first apartment and we cobbled together a colorful mix from all different places. At Target, you could walk in and easily transport yourself into your own personal oasis.

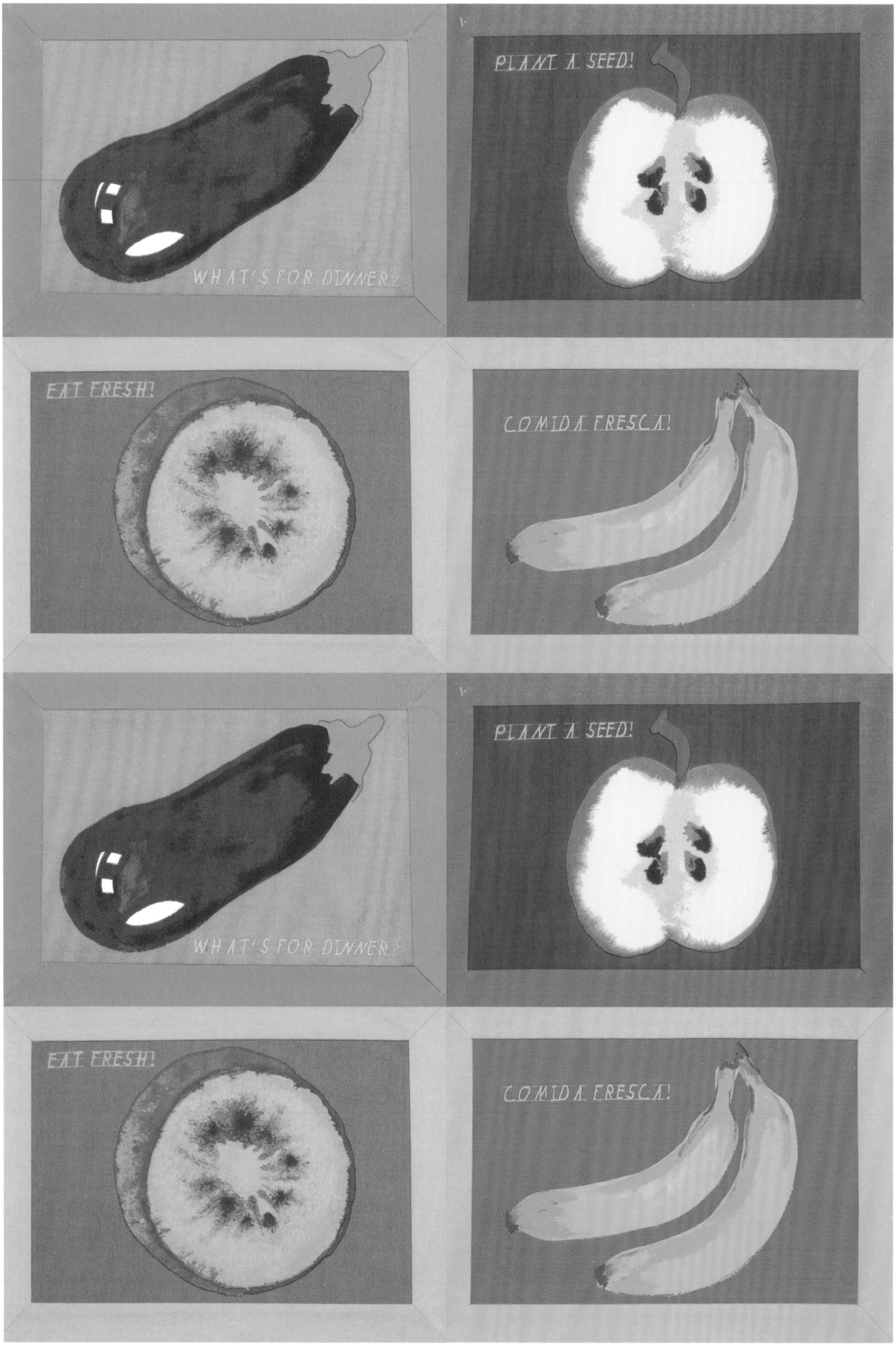
WHAT'S FOR DINNER?
PLANT A SEED!
EAT FRESH!
COMIDA FRESCA!
WHAT'S FOR DINNER?
PLANT A SEED!
EAT FRESH!
COMIDA FRESCA!

Marcus Samuelsson
2010

Marcus Samuelsson, Culinary Mastermind, Cooks Up His Debut Kitchenware

Marcus Samuelsson is a Harlem legend from the new school. His beloved dining spot, Red Rooster—which opened in 2010 on 125th Street—is surrounded by urban histories, music and iconic American cuisine. In the 20s, venue-restaurants like the Lenox Lounge and the still-open Minton's Playhouse were celebrated haunts for a host of brilliant minds—think Cab Calloway, Billie Holliday and John Coltrane—at a time when segregation prevented them from performing elsewhere. Samuelsson is part of that lineage: an award-winning chef, writer (four cookbooks and the memoir *Yes, Chef*), and food sustainability advocate.

Ethiopian-born and Swedish-raised, Samuelsson moved to New York in 1994, where he merged formal European techniques with flavors plucked from across the African continent. Red Rooster offers an elevated take on classics like fried chicken and jambalaya, incorporating left-field ingredients without sacrificing the food's timeless appeal.

For our Harlem designer series, he added kitchenware design to his skillset. Produce-covered aprons, towels, and oven mitts are dotted with kaleidoscopic bananas, crunchy peppers, and, in playful schoolhouse lettering, encouragement like "125th Street SPICY"—and the very resonant "Harlem's FRESH!"

Our design team recalls Samuelsson's crayon aesthetic was inspired by his work in schools—wanting to make healthy food appealing for local kids. (A portion of the proceeds were donated to Harlem's public school libraries.) To celebrate, around the time of the launch, the chef invited Target's lead designer to his home and cooked him a meal.

Marcus Samuelsson, photographed by Kwaku Alston

Opposite:
Fabric placemats by Marcus Samuelsson for Target

HARLEm

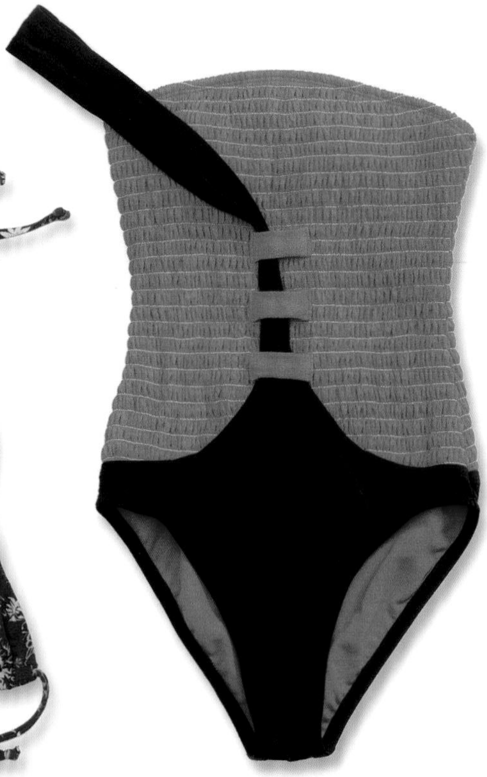

El Museo
ToLeDo

ToLeDo

Art Meets Life with Harlem Heroes Isabel and Ruben Toledo

When we launched Target in Harlem—our first-ever storefront in Manhattan—we partnered with a handful of local greats on prismatic capsule lines to celebrate the major milestone, including Isabel and Ruben Toledo and Chef Marcus Samuelsson. Our intentions were simple: highlight some of our favorite Harlem talent, while giving back to the community. 5% of profits from each collection's sales were donated to a neighborhood non-profit, chosen by the artists.

Isabel and Ruben Toledo are one of those legendary New York artist couples. They emerged as twin creative forces after a lucky run-in with drag artist Joey Arias at the Fiorucci store, back in 1977. Legend has it that Arias showed their portfolio to Andy Warhol—he was also hanging out in-store—who championed their work. "What matters is to have free expression always, which we picked up from Andy immediately," Ruben told *The Cut*. While Isabel and Ruben often work together, they each have their own practice—Isabel is a designer by trade, although she calls herself a "seamstress," Ruben an artist. In reality, their processes are enmeshed; each is constantly in conversation with the other. Their skills range across disciplines—Ruben is a painter, illustrator, and glass-blower, who hand-blows sculptures in Dale Chihuly's factory. Isabel is a fashion designer; she's dressed luminaries like Michelle Obama in her trademark sculptural outfits—the new First Lady even wore one of her dresses to her husband's inauguration.

The Toledos' collection for us was their first-ever retail line, but there were firsts for Target as well. A soft, marigold beach towel—adorned with a psychedelic artwork of a woman in a coiled African neckpiece—involved finding a new printing technique; we later used it on towels made with Peter Pilotto. There were other aquatic pieces: bikinis bedecked with swirling black-and-white formations or patterns resembling coral, a tightly ruched one-piece in red and black and a towel with an enormous butterfly.

Isabel and Ruben Toledo, photographed by Deborah Feingold

Opposite: A selection of images from the couple's Target collection

MUSEUM OF ICE CREAM
Cherrylicious
PIÑATA
CHURRO CHURRO
CHOCOLATE CRUSH

Museum of
Ice Cream
2018

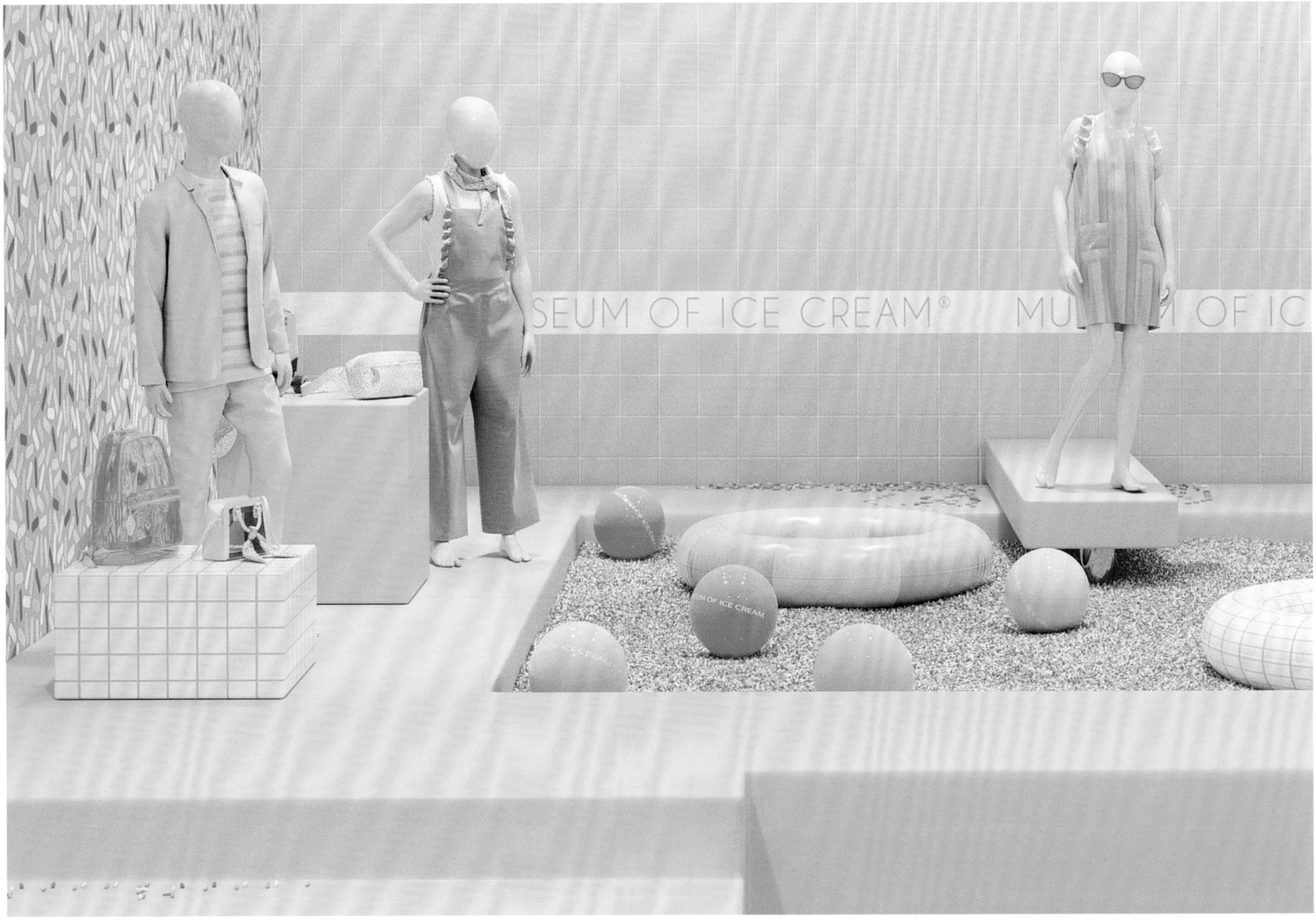
SEUM OF ICE CREAM®

Museum of Ice Cream for Target campaign image

Opposite: A 360-degree shoppable room developed for our collaboration, in homage to the multi-room, sensory experience at the Museum of Ice Cream

Previous spread: The Museum of Ice Cream's first pints of ice cream, sold exclusively at Target, in seven flavors

Dreaming Big with the Museum of Ice Cream

When Maryellis Bunn co-launched the first Museum of Ice Cream in New York with Manish Vora—an experiential, selfie-friendly maze filled with sprinkle pools and tasting stations—she drew on fantastical childhood dreams to design the interiors. It's no surprise that her immersive installation captured our designers' hearts and taste buds too. "When our team visited the first Museum of Ice Cream in New York City, they instantly knew it was something special," said our Executive Vice President, Mark Tritton.

Through sheer force of imagination, Bunn's been able to manifest her dreams into reality. Case in point: the fantastical ice cream flavors she made for us when we partnered in 2018, including Nana Banana, Cherrylicious, Chocolate Crush, Churro Churro and Vanillionaire. She even created a line of pastel kids clothing to pair them with, plus roller skates and banana-covered backpacks. In tribute to making the impossible real, she suggests the fantastical ice cream flavors she'd make if nothing stood in the way. (Maybe we'll make them together in the future.)

Fly Cream It's simple: the feeling of flying captured in a pint filled with the fluffiest clouds.

Memory Lane Evoke a memory through the power of classic vanilla sprinkled with nostalgia.

Play D'oh Build, shape and mold your own world with the unique dough bites.

Mood Cream The psychedelic color and flavor profiles shift to match your current emotions and thoughts.

ET Cone Home A portal is created when eaten that allows you to be transported anywhere—even to Mars.

Askov
Finlayson
#TeamNorthxTarget

PUMA

NORTH
Askov
Finlayson
NORTH

Askov
Finlayson
2018

Northern Exposure: Adventuring through Cooler Climes with Askov Finlayson

Minnesota-bred clothing brand Askov Finlayson—its name a combination of two small towns in the state sharing a freeway exit—isn't satisfied with the Midwest's mild-mannered reputation. The brand's founders, Eric and Andrew Dayton, believe their native region can lead the way on issues of climate change, so they donate 110% of the carbon cost of producing their wares towards climate change solutions. (Their mission statement is "Keep the North Cold.")

It's all about making a mark while tapping into Midwest values, like self-reliance. They even want to change the region's name: since its 2011 inception, Askov Finlayson has attempted to rebrand the whole area as "the North," emblazoning the words across sturdy coats, wool socks, and snappy backpacks, along with a suite of outdoor gear.

In 2018, the Super Bowl took place in Minneapolis. Its slogan, "Bold North," was partly inspired by Askov Finlayson. In January, ahead of the big game—and as a way to celebrate what makes Minnesota cool during its most freezing month—we partnered with the brand on a collection of more than 50 pieces that included woolen gloves, beanies, and cozy blankets. It was perfect game-ready gear, designed for backyard Super Bowl streaming or outdoor adventures, whatever the weather.

Along with other socially conscious collaborators like TOMS and FEED, Askov Finlayson have found a way to build progress into their business model without sacrificing design. "We continue to be motivated by the belief that our part of the country has something unique to offer," said co-founder Eric Dayton. "I think you can find that spirit in the quality and functionality of the products—up here, your clothing has a job to do, especially in winter. But you also don't have to trade function for style, and this collection delivers both."

Mittens by Askov Finlayson for Target

Opposite: Askov Finlayson's launch at Theodore Wirth Park in Minneapolis, a pop-up event complete with snow tubing, dog sledding, jumbo bubble hockey, and wintery Super Bowl installations for over 2,000 guests

5. 9x14" GRAPHIC OR LETTERS TRAY $12.99 each

6. 12x12" BUTTERFLIES OR BIRD TRAY $16.99 each

1. LOVE OR BUTTERFLY PLATE $5.99 each

John Derian
2008+2010

7. BUTTERFLY PAPERWEIGHTS $9.99 each

CHARM &
AND
MOMENTS.
8. LARGE BUTTERFLY SHADOW BOX $16.99

Remixing History: The Curious World of John Derian

A disembodied eye. An artichoke. A freshly frosted fruit tart. Images of flora and fauna seemingly plucked straight from a 19th century taxonomy book. John Derian's whimsical objects would look right at home in a centuries-old stately house, but the New York-based decoupage artist has a knack for infusing surreal iconography into the things we use every day. (Decoupage, by the way, is the art of decorating an object by covering it with paper cutouts—often taken from old books and documents—then adding gold leaf and clever paint effects.)

That fruit tart? It's actually a candle. That finely drawn eye? Printed on a tote bag. The artichoke? Collaged onto a small tray. A love of both antiques and the natural world are key to unlocking the method behind Derian's magic—but chance plays a role too. The designer once told *The Guardian*, "I find things. I let things happen."

We've collaborated with the mastermind for years on home décor items—think wall art, journals, ceramic mugs and melamine tableware—plus limited-edition holiday offerings, like layered gift wrap and ornaments. Every object is charged with history: a place for the eyes to discover and explore. "What's interesting to me," Derian says, "is that 99% of the imagery I use was [originally] used for instructional purposes. It's all educational, telling stories about things from the past we still connect with today. I was recently obsessed with a pile of book pages from the 1600s showing thousands-of-years-old coins, shells, and even mummies. It's a little like being an archeologist—making discoveries and learning more about the past."

For us, the designer loved being able to share his love for 19th century imagery on a large scale. "One image we used was an interior of an empty room painted pink," he recalls. "Another was a 17th-century plan of an Italian garden. Anything maze-like I find fascinating."

John Derian, photographed by Matthew Williams

Opposite: In these John Derian for Target images, butterflies are perched atop collaged book pages printed on melamine plates

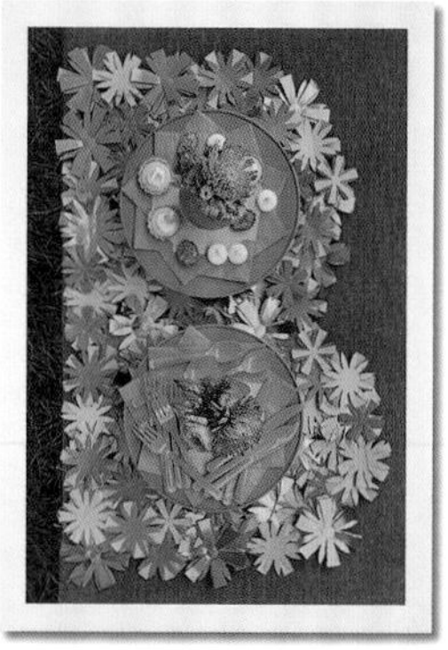
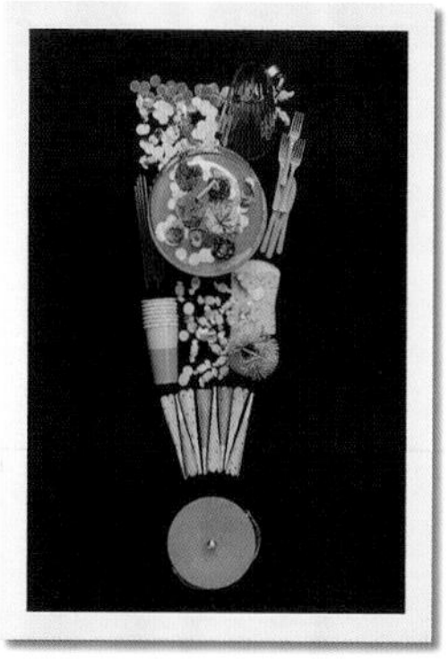
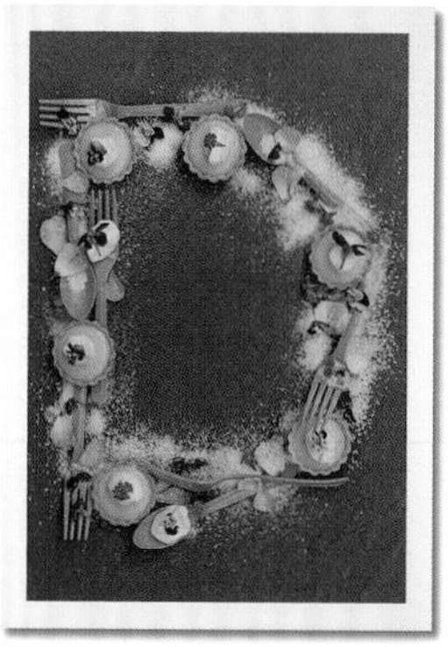

HELLO
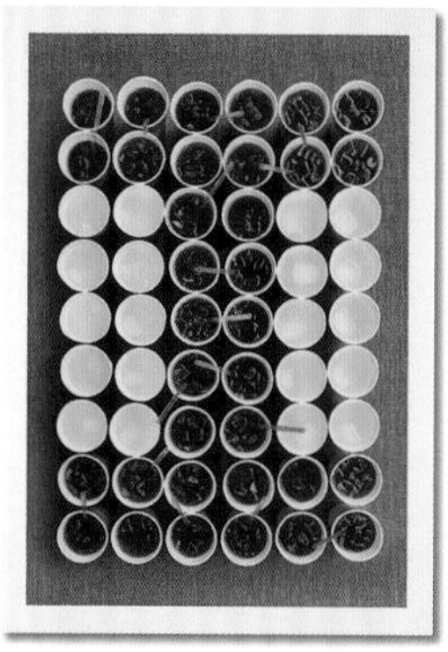

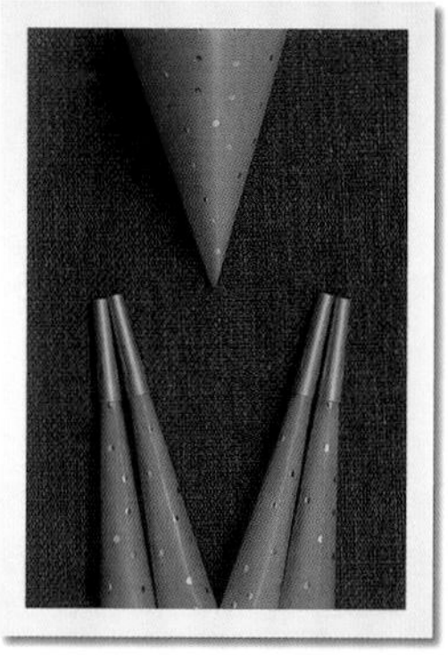

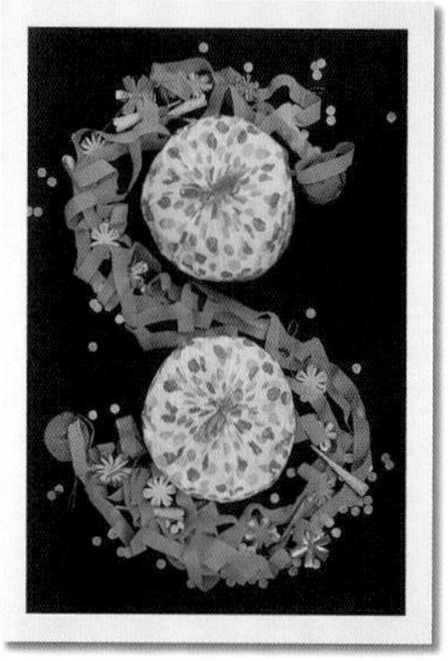

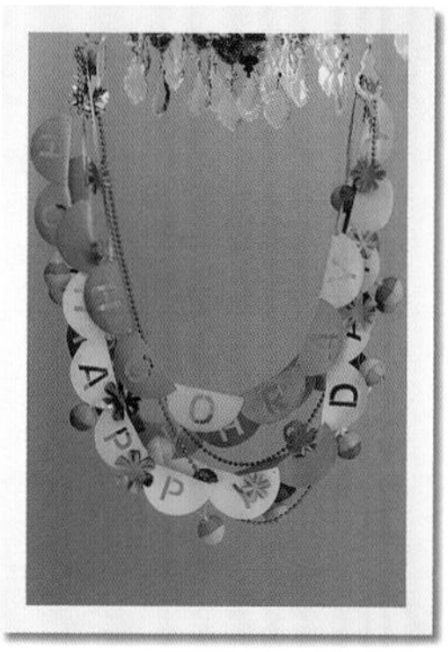

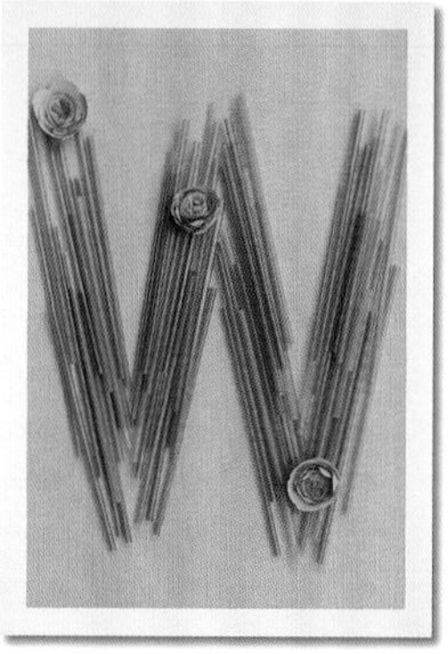

Oh Joy!
2014-2017

The Oh Joy! Design Empire Built with Colorful Crafty Charm

Thirteen million people can't be wrong. That's the staggering number of followers that home furnishings designer Joy Cho has amassed on Pinterest, where she's the most followed person in the world. Her precisely curated boards cover everything from mood palettes for her dream house to guides for dressing with a baby bump.

Cho is also the brains behind design studio Oh Joy!, who we've partnered with for years on everything from pet products and pillows to string lights and confetti—the essentials required to transform any living space into an inviting oasis. After launching Oh Joy! in 2005, Cho became one of the people with the most sway over the colorful, crafty aesthetic that's dominated social media and real life home design over the past decade. She's been recognized by *Time* magazine as one of the 30 most influential people online for two years in a row, described as the leader of a "lifestyle empire." She's also written several books, including titles like *Oh Joy!: 60 Ways to Create & Give Joy*, packed with tips on adding vibrancy to any home.

In a recent collection for us, Cho brings joy-sparking details to household objects. Delicate single-flower vases in shades of ochre and emerald pair with green bowls elevated by a scalloped rim. A gold band transforms colorful glasses into something almost royal, while tasteful cake-topper letters proclaim HOORAY in bright shades. It's all you need to throw the most Instagrammable birthday party ever—just bring your own cake.

Joy Cho, photographed by Nicki Sebastian

Opposite:
Oh Joy! for Target collaboration with Pinterest. Alphabet postcards included fun party tips

MINI

Harajuku
Mini
2011-2012

THE MINI'S
DANCE TO YOUR OWN BEAT

When in Tokyo: Holidaying in Harajuku with Gwen Stefani

Goth. Punk. Schoolgirl. Sailor. While these might sound like fashion stereotypes of American high schools, they're also style staples of Harajuku culture, which inspired Gwen Stefani's Harajuku Mini line for us, debuting in 2011.

The central Tokyo neighborhood of Harajuku has long been a beloved shopping destination for locals and tourists. It's home to multi-floor, multi-sensory Japanese malls, themed cafes, and couture shops, all on the same high-energy street. Since the 1980s, it's been a meet-up spot for Japanese youth shunning their required school uniforms and opting for wilder looks—as well as the tourists who love to take pictures of them doing it.

Harajuku looks are ever-evolving (that's fashion, after all). Some mainstays include *lolita* (frilly Victorian formal wear), *fairy kei* (pastel Care Bear palettes), *gyaru* (tanned, Western-influenced looks), *decora* (super-layered accessories), and—most influential to the tartan plaid and mini-backpacks in Stefani's line—punk and *kogal* (schoolgirl).

Stefani's looks catered to infants, toddlers and tweens in search of statement-making beach and back-to-school styles: be it video game graphics, safari prints or all-over nautical prints. The designer knows better than most that the identities you can create through clothes are endless.

Gwen Stefani, photographed by Michele Laurita

Previous spread: Harajuku Mini for Target, photographed by Michele Laurita

Opposite: Still from Stefani's Target collection

HARAJUKU
MINI

80s teens in Harajuku loved the DIY aesthetic—all safety pins and tartan—pioneered by 70s punks in London and New York. In Stefani's line, it's softened with frothy ballet underskirts

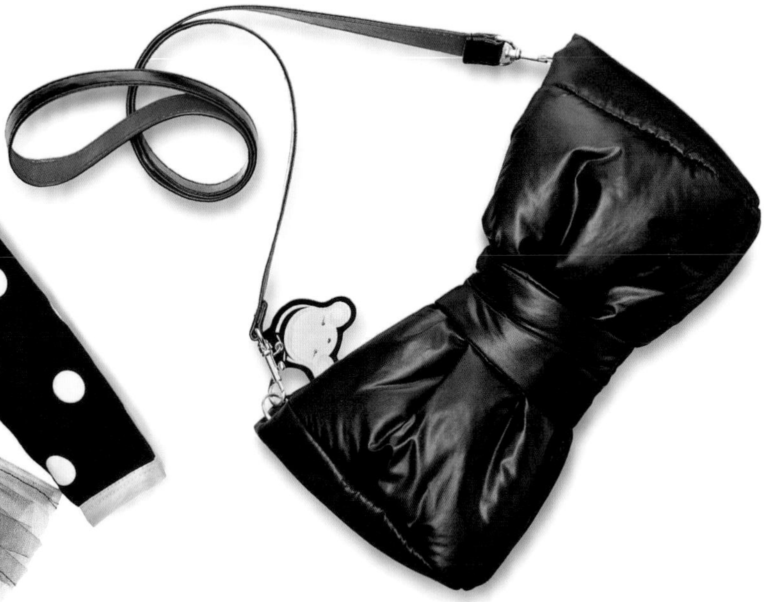

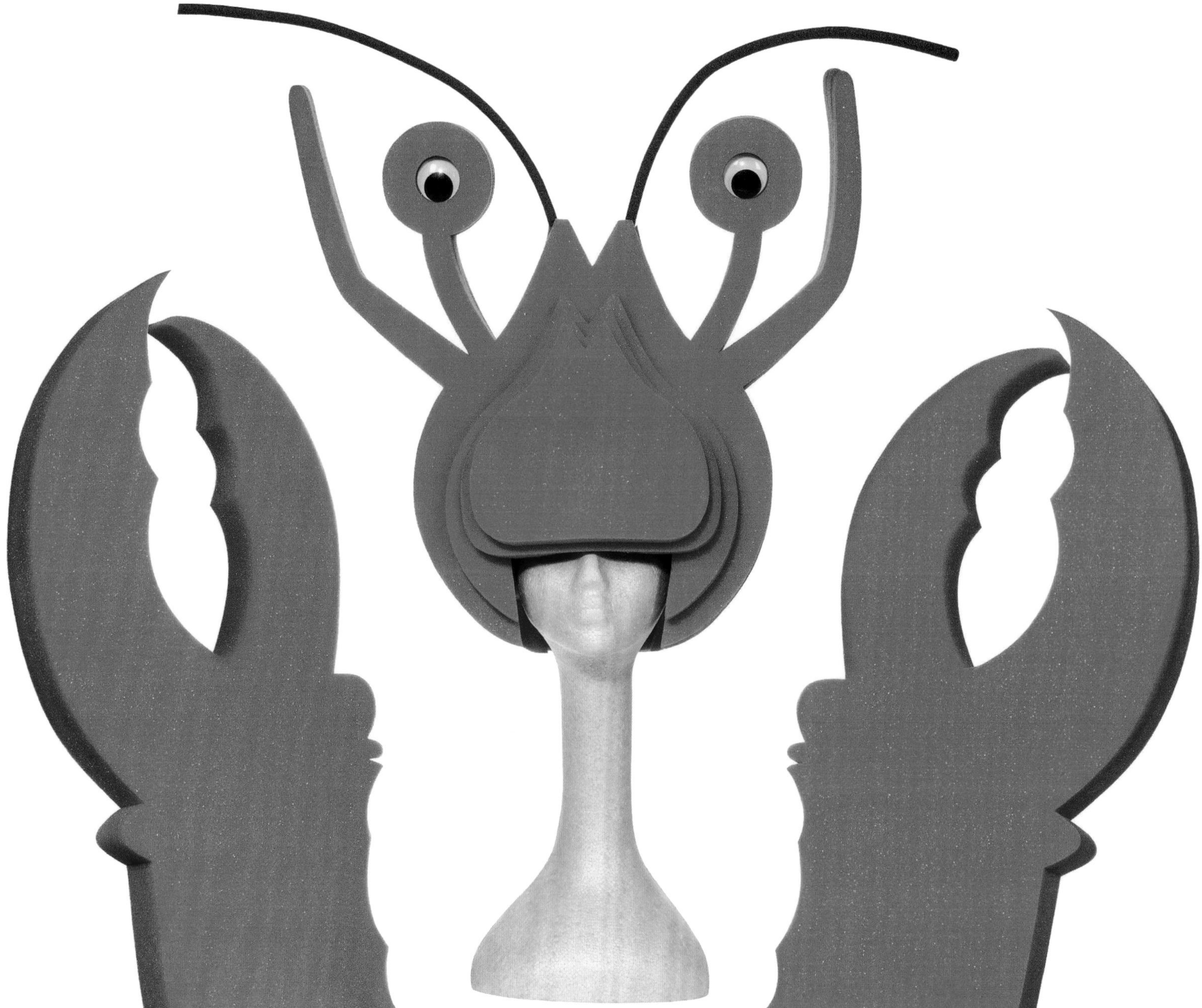

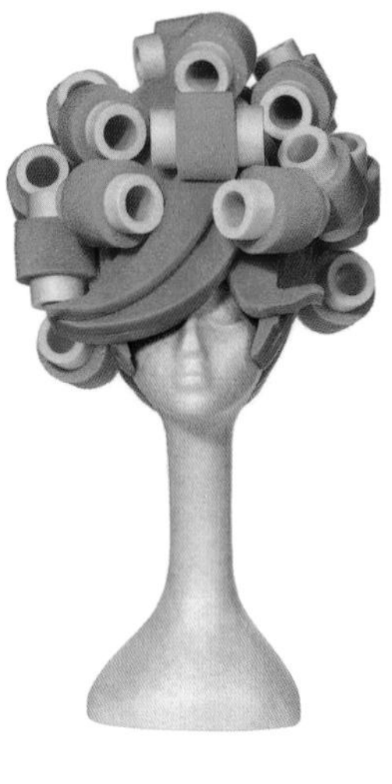

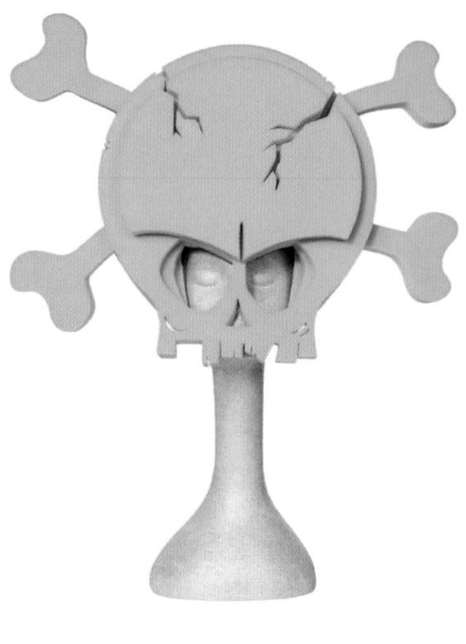

The Wig Is Up: Making Chris March's Head-Turning Bouffants

Chris March has never been the type to avoid risks when it comes to avant-garde design. As a contestant on Season 4 of Bravo's *Project Runway*, March created an entire collection incorporating hundreds of safety pins and real human hair (inspiring an all-time classic Tim Gunn observation: "You've been living in the monkey house, Chris.")

March—who grew up in the Bay Area and started out creating gigantic hats for the San Francisco production of *Beach Blanket Babylon*—may not have taken home the season's top spot, but his fantastical visions and natural charisma charmed audiences worldwide. One of the show's most popular alumni, he parlayed his appearance into a successful career designing costumes for the likes of Madonna, Prince, Cirque du Soleil, and Beyoncé, whose *I Am...* tour featured his work. He even starred in his own reality show, *Mad Fashion*, on Bravo in 2011.

In 2013, March crafted a collection of marvelously oversize foam wigs for our Halloween product line. "I've been designing costumes and wigs for more than 20 years," he explained at the time, "And my new collection with Target is so beyond my wildest dreams we couldn't call it anything but Big Fun." He created eight looks based on dramatic archetypes: the elaborate Medusa model featured a tangle of hissing green snakes, while the striking Greaser offered swooping 50s chic. There's also the Starlet, a bright yellow ode to bombshells like Marilyn Monroe, and the Witch, a tenacious black and white number with shades of Elvira. They're custom-built costumes, allowing their wearers to pack an entire dramatic identity into a few ounces of colorful foam.

The wigs exemplified March's ability to balance smart design with fizzy theatrics. He is, after all, a consummate entertainer, imbuing the simplest of garments with contagious playfulness. That exuberance was captured in the outfit March wore to the launch party for the collection: glitter-dusted overalls, a custom T-shirt reading "WIG BOY," and, of course, a flamboyant, towering wig.

Chris March at his Target launch party, photographed by Astrid Stawiarz, 2013

Opposite: A selection of wigs from Chris March for Target collection

Luella Bartley, photographed by Harry Borden/ Contour, 2001

Opposite and next spread: A selection of items from the Luella Bartley for Target collection

Punk and Playful the Iconic English Style of Luella Bartley

A fashion household name in her native UK, Luella Bartley kick-started her career in journalism as a fashion editor at *British Vogue* and the *Evening Standard* before diving head-first into design. Since transitioning from keyboard to needle, Bartley has worked with brands like Mulberry, Marc Jacobs, Calvin Klein, and her own self-titled label, Luella—known for its psychedelic take on prim-and-proper English style, with patchworked fabrics, pompoms, satin bows and plenty of pockets.

Bartley is as eclectic as her hopscotch career suggests. In 2006, we joined forces to bring a new kind of style to the States: preppy polos and pops of color, moto jackets and mini skirts and strapless gingham dresses. It was English eccentricity meets soft, school-girl silhouettes.

After our collaboration launched, Bartley's career continued to climb. She outfitted the coolest of creative women: Chloë Sevigny, Kate Nash, and Amy Winehouse. In 2007, Bartley returned to London where she opened her first store. In 2008 after launching a limited-edition bag collection in Hong Kong, Bartley was named Designer of the Year by the British Fashion Council. And in 2010 she was appointed Member of the Order of the British Empire. It turns out everyone is charmed by Bartley's brand of fun—even the Queen of England.

Bartley's collection abounded with pop-infused cherry patterns, hearts and skulls—emblazoned across everything from totes to coin purses to clutches.

These designers look for beauty everywhere—in art, film, music, nature, in the texture of certain fabrics—but most of all, in the confident, artful women who often become their muses. For some, like the ever-joyful Isaac Mizrahi, fashion is a way to celebrate classic forms and bring luxury to women everywhere. For others, like Jason Wu and Altuzarra, romance comes from the way garments dress the female body—be it elegant pleats or the power that comes from a structured knee-high boot. In the world of romantics, fashion can be anything: pure escapism or a conversation with the world. But mostly, it's about generosity, tenderness, and love.

Isaac Mizrahi
2003-2009

Jason Wu
2012

Victoria Beckham
2017

Altuzarra
2014

Proenza Schouler
2007

Kate Young
2013

Neiman Marcus
2012

Phillip Lim
2013

Zac Posen
2010

Jonathan Saunders
2008

Erin Fetherston
2007

Romantics

Isaac
Mizrahi
2003-2009

How Isaac Mizrahi Brought Downtown Sleek to America

"Oh hi! I'm Isaac Mizrahi, wait 'til you see these clothes I've designed for Target," says the legendary designer-turned-cabaret star, beaming ear to ear as he leaps down a staircase and enters a showroom buzzing with activity. "Cheap, affordable, divine!"

This is how a 2003 ad for our long-running partnership with Mizrahi kicks off. It's a fascinating time capsule: a peek into one of the first designer collaborations with a mass retailer in America. The ad embraces the idea of connection between the frenzy of downtown New York and the charm of small towns everywhere. To drive the point home, Mizrahi hops in the back seat of a yellow taxi cab that zooms past fields of corn. "It's, like, Fifth Avenue meets Main Street USA," he declares. "It's a big country. You're gonna need some great shoes!"

Our collections with Mizrahi—spanning bridal and ready to wear—walked a line between universal wearability and cutting-edge cool. Mizrahi updated classic, comfortable silhouettes with unusual, edgy materials: lavender suede jackets, silver trench coats, and strappy faux-snake heels. At the end of that 2003 spot, we see the designer sitting in a diner; he snaps his fingers like a fairy godmother and a waitress' apron transforms into a glossy dress shirt. "I love you in pink," he says. "Gorgeous!"

Deemed one of the most successful fashion partnerships in history, Mizrahi's relationship with us was a powerful meeting of the minds; we share an approachable, amusing, and high-impact visual language. Before the deal was inked, Mizrahi sold his collection at high-end luxury stores. We gave him the chance to reinvent his sleek, minimalist couture for a broader audience. In doing so, he created a new kind of apparel—one that appealed to women looking for fashion at once wearable and wallet-friendly.

In another gloriously "Isaac" TV spot for the collection, Mizrahi plays piano and sings Judy Garland's classic ballad "I Believe in You." The notion of Mizrahi—a beloved fixture of cosmopolitan cool—encouraging women everywhere to access their inner diva proved transformative; Mizrahi's whimsical color palettes and structured silhouettes would soon be spotted all over America.

Portrait of Isaac Mizrahi

Opposite: Isaac Mizrahi, photographed by Nick Waplington

ISAAC MIZRAHI
FOR TARGET

Space age:
a shimmering coat
by Isaac Mizrahi
for Target, plus a
minimalist silver
clock sporting
statement hands,
from Mizrahi's
foray into home
furnishings

SAA

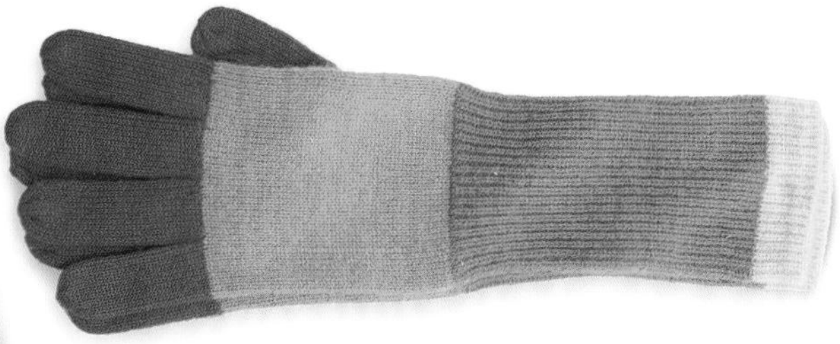

ZRAHI

5th AVE
MAIN ST

Even before I knew I was designing, I was absorbing my mother's design thinking and ferocity.

In Conversation with Isaac Mizrahi

Interview by Trey Taylor

If Charles Worth invented high fashion, then Isaac Mizrahi brought it to the masses with his wildly successful, half-decade Target collaboration. Raised on a diet of secular Jewish fashion, the incipient designer would put on puppet shows at birthday parties in exchange for money. His fledgling business taught him how to sew properly, by hand. His father, Zeke, who worked in the New York rag trade, helped Mizrahi pick out his first sewing machine. From that point on, his boldly colored, minimalist designs would spring from the presser foot and into the closets of Manhattan's upper crust.

At a trunk show for New York department store Bergdorf Goodman in 1987, Mizrahi presented his first collection. It was lauded by the fashion press and scooped up by several high-end retailers, setting him on a path to success. Once his father passed away, Mizrahi took his inheritance and set up a studio on SoHo's Greene Street. At the height of his label's success, Mizrahi was the subject of the documentary *Unzipped*, which followed the making of his Fall 1994 collection. It too propelled Mizrahi into the dizzying heights of celebrity. Traipsing through his studio at any given moment were any one of the Big Five supermodels: Linda, Christy, Cindy, Naomi, or Claudia.

In 2002, Mizrahi began a fruitful partnership with Target, meting out affordable chic to Americans everywhere. To call it a triumph would be reductive: it generated $300 million each year in revenue. His designs—sleek slingbacks and cute corduroy dresses—remain among Target's most beloved collaborations. As if his design nous weren't enough, Mizrahi moonlights as a cabaret singer and judge on *Project Runway: All Stars*. He's put it all in writing for a memoir and, looking back, he wouldn't change a thing.

TREY TAYLOR I read that your father gave you a sewing machine when you were a child?

ISAAC MIZRAHI Yeah, he did. When I was about 13, I bought my first sewing machine with my own money. I saved up this money babysitting—my father helped me pick out the machine. It was an antique. He was right in telling me that older machines were better. He had a manufacturing [business]: a few different factories across the country and eventually in the Dominican Republic and Hong Kong. But when I was a kid, he had some of the most amazing sewing machines stored in the basement of the house—two of them—a straight stitch machine and an old overcast machine. They were like this hidden treasure in the basement. I started making puppets when I was very young, like seven or eight years old. And I learned to sew by hand in order to make them. I made all of my puppets on that machine, I made the first clothes that I ever made for anyone on it, you know? My father was very instrumental in all of that.

TT What do you credit as giving you your official start in designing?

IM I can't remember a time when I wasn't *thinking* design thoughts. Even before I knew I was designing, I was absorbing my mother's design thinking and ferocity. She was a very chic person, and she had real rigorous ideas about stuff. She was not your typical middle-class stylish person. She saw herself as this kind of noble fashion luminary in the community where we grew up. She took that responsibility, if you will, really seriously. I picked up on that, and she taught me things. It wasn't just about [leading by] example; she also spoke about it.

I started making puppets when I was very young, like seven or eight years old. And I learned to sew by hand in order to make them.

Isaac Mizrahi, photographed by Christopher Lane, 2005

TT When?
IM We had these Saturday breakfasts when I was a kid, and we conversed about a lot of things, including style and clothes. That was my favorite subject. It was an early education on the subject of style and fashion.

TT When did you stop having these breakfasts together?
IM Oh, [they took place] as long as I lived in my mom's house. I moved out when I was 20. They became fewer and farther between, after I got to late high school age. Once I started college, I don't remember many of them. And these breakfasts were about cooking, too! I used to make scrambled eggs, and I learned how to sauté vegetables. It was a crazy, wonderful thing between us.

TT When you were approached to make the documentary *Unzipped* and have your life filmed, what was your initial reaction?
IM Well, it wasn't even so much a reaction as much as like, a collective idea to make the thing. It was this idea because of how fabulous my studio was at the time. Just this thought of all these movie stars and all these models running in and out of the space. You'd have to be crazy not to get the idea to film it.

TT How did it come to be?
IM It was me, my associate Nina Santisi and my boyfriend at the time, Douglas Keeve, who was transitioning into filmmaking from being a successful fashion photographer—we all had this idea. And then, we got the financing to make it. Eventually, it got made because of our perseverance. But it wasn't some crazy production. It was us. We were the producers. It was like a home movie.

TT I remember that one scene where you were talking about your process: how you soak up all this inspiration and then create a hundred sketches. Is that still the case?
IM Well, I mean, I don't really do those kinds of collections [now], so it wouldn't be the case. Now, I make very accessible clothes. Something I don't understand is mood boards—I would never have referred to anyone else's clothes. But one can fool oneself into believing they're in their own little world, that no one is going to see this. It's like you go into this crazy little room of creativity, and you convince yourself that it's just for you to be looking at—no one else. That is what I do. I pretend that I'm the only person who's going to see something. That's the only way I can start.

TT Do you feel as though you had a hand in democratizing fashion when you began your collaboration with Target?
IM Yeah. I have committed myself to the thought that I wasn't standing for couture but for democratizing fashion. I had this deal with Target whereby they were the real distributor of my clothes. The only other deal I had was with Bergdorf [Goodman], and I felt that was a very important part of the whole thing.

TT How did the idea for "High Low" come about?
IM [The executives at Target and I] eventually landed on "High Low." It was not a phrase that was out there. Maybe we didn't coin it, but I feel I came up with it separately from anyone else. People had been thinking about it. You had Gianni Versace showing crown jewels with jeans. I was doing T-shirts with ball-gown skirts. I was actually committing to it in a way. If I didn't invent it, I was the one who committed to it first—before Karl Lagerfeld, rest in peace, did anything with H&M or Vera Wang did anything with Kohl's. It wasn't just the idea. It was the execution, too.

TT I was watching your Target commercials. There's one where you sing "I Believe."
IM Yes I did. I've been doing cabaret for quite some time. I think I remember it happening at the launch of the [collection]. Late 2001. We hosted this party at the Rainbow Room in tandem with a pop-up shop at 30 Rockefeller Plaza. It was literally the second pop-up shop in the world. I didn't come up with the idea. One of the ad executives I guess had heard about it or something like that, and I was thrilled at the idea. There were literally lines around the block at 30 Rock. It looked like my instinct was right. But the idea is that at 30 Rock I got my band to play, and I got up and did a few numbers and someone said, "Oh, why don't we use that for your commercial." And I thought, that's a great idea, you know? It wasn't the first ad—it was maybe the second ad that we did.

TT Your lines generated over $300 million in sales each year for five years at Target.
IM It was a giant business, and I think it was even closer to $400 million by the time we finished.

TT When you reflect upon that success that you had, how do you feel?
IM It makes me feel like my life means something.

Baby
Bebés
Home Storage
BATTERY
CENTER
25.00
HUGGIES
HUGGIES
TARGET

Stills from the Isaac Mizrahi for Target TV commercials

Opposite:
Campaign imagery, featuring Carmen Dell'Orefice

Jason Wu
2012

JASON WU

Jason Wu: From Presidential Style to American Girl in Paris

Only a few designers have had the opportunity to visually define a First Lady's time in the Oval Office—and Jason Wu is among them. Over the past decade, his work for Michelle Obama helped cement her sophisticated sartorial reputation; in turn, she championed his work, bestowing upon him the global recognition he enjoys today. In 2008, she chose one of his dresses to wear to her first Inaugural Ball, a show-stopping, intricate white number in lace. At the time, he was only 26, and had started his eponymous label just two years prior. He'd go on to dress her for countless public appearances, including the second Inaugural Ball.

"Under the intense scrutiny of the brightest spotlight imaginable, I felt confident, beautiful, and comfortable in my own skin when wearing his clothes," Obama told *Interview* magazine. "But I'm drawn to Jason not just because of his remarkable talent, but also because of his warmth of spirit, kind heart, and inspiring personal story. When we talk about the American Dream, we're talking about people like him."

Born in Taiwan and raised in Vancouver, Wu's life in design began when his mother gave him a sewing machine. He used it to dress his dolls in custom clothes, teaching himself to create intricately detailed mini outfits. Wu debuted his first ready-to-wear collection in 2007, with an emphasis on sleek tailoring. "I create clothes for women who not only are fiercely fashionable but also own their power and femininity," said Wu.

In 2012, Wu teamed up with us for a collection based around the concept of an American girl in Paris. Think expertly tailored canvas skirts cast in sky blue, ribbon-topped blouses, striped red jersey dresses (a Parisian staple, in an all-American palette) and the simplest of T-shirts. The collection also featured an adorable mascot: Milu, a mischievous ribbon-wearing cat who appears on a tote. In the accompanying campaign film, Wu himself makes a cameo too—sketching in his design studio. He sketches Milu into being, who magically leaps off the page and knocks over Wu's new creations, serving as a manifestation of the designer's playfulness and wit. Wu was set on the collection concept as soon as we approached him. As always, his instincts were spot on—it sold out almost instantly.

Jason Wu, photographed by Dan King

Opposite: A look from the Jason Wu for Target collection

Previous spread and this page: Jason Wu for Target campaign photographed by Tim Gutt

Opposite:
A selection of looks from the 50-plus piece Jason Wu for Target collection

Victoria
Beckham
2017

Motherhood to Modern Style: The Legacy of Victoria Beckham

Victoria Beckham—former Spice Girl, 2000s model to Dolce and Gabbana and Roberto Cavalli, and founder of one of the world's most respected contemporary fashion labels—doesn't need any help to confirm her place as one of the UK's coolest visionaries. Since its launch in 2008, Beckham's label has modernized women's ready-to-wear with collections praised for their chic sensibility. Sarah Mower of *Vogue* has said her secret weapon is "this unpretentious pragmatism backed up by interesting, deftly chosen fabrics."

In 2011, she launched Victoria, Victoria Beckham, a more affordable take on her namesake line. That same year, she was named Designer Brand of the Year in the UK at the British Fashion Awards. She's designed in every category imaginable—bags, shoes, accessories, and eyewear. She's collaborated in beauty, fragrance, and sportswear categories, and in 2017 launched a family-friendly line with us that included her debut into kidswear.

Taking cues from both her own style and the connection she shares with her daughter, Harper, the pieces were infused with an energetic elegance. From playful prints to scalloped edges, silky sets to fitted trousers, Victoria Beckham for Target didn't need to try hard to turn heads. Instead, it brought fantastical fashion to the everyday for women (and girls) alike.

Stills from the Victoria Beckham for Target TV commercial

Opposite: Victoria Beckham, photographed by Pamela Hanson, 2017

On launch day, we had a stealth plan with our sizes and styles picked out. "Divide and conquer," we'd said, knowing crazy fashionistas would be flocking to the racks.

Elise Giannasi, Victoria Beckham fan

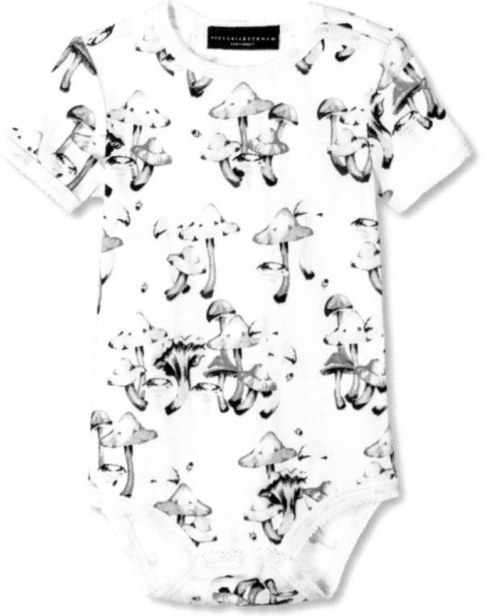

VICTORIA BECKHAM
VB

Hauler If You Hear Me: A Victoria Beckham Superfan Takes Us Behind the Scenes of YouTube Hauls

On the release of Victoria Beckham for Target, YouTuber and "collaboration fanatic" Jessica Flores—self-described as a "fashion-loving, beauty-obsessed, DIY project-making Latina mom from New York City"—released a haul video, one of her biggest. In it, she runs through $500 of merchandise, analyzing each piece thoughtfully, be it printed blankets, a satin dress with a ruffle hem, or coloring books or a see-through raincoat for her daughter. "I love the idea of having a clear one," she says, "because sometimes she's got a really pretty dress on and you don't want to cover it up!" Flores thinks the vlog connected so well with her audience because it was intergenerational: "The collection was mainly for women and girls, and shoppers were eager to share ... what they were able to get for themselves and their daughters."

Flores started posting haul videos regularly after the popularity of her first one, another designer collaboration haul. "That is when I realized I could gain views and subscribers simply by sharing what I do and love in my day-to-day life," Flores recalled. "More so, I could share tips and help others decide if something is right for them. My haul videos continue to be some of my most popular content."

On YouTube, haulers of all ages share details of bargains and mega-buys with unabashed zeal. It's impossible to pinpoint exactly when the trend started, but uploads go back as far as 2007. In 2010, it was reported that a quarter of a million haul videos had been uploaded. YouTubers like CookieSwirlC and AlishaMarieVlogs have used the medium to gush about their hauls from our stores to the tune of millions of views. Haul videos connect so effectively because they transform what used to be a solitary activity—shopping—into a communal one. Everyone can share in the satisfaction of finding clothing or homeware that makes life feel a little more beautiful. Haulers in the scene aren't competitive with each other, says Flores; instead, the hunt sparks camaraderie. "I enjoy watching other creators do hauls because, like many consumers and viewers of haul videos, I want to see what's out there. I have certainly bonded with my viewers in the comment section over what we were able to get our hands on and our thoughts on the collection."

Hauling isn't all fun and games, though. Flores explains that there's plenty of prep work behind each video she makes, starting with the research required before a collaboration like Beckham's drops. "I stalk Target's website and any news articles that feature the collections," she says. "I look at every single piece and find the prices. I then create a wishlist with every item I'm mildly interested in with the price. I make sure I have a good estimate of the amount of money I could spend and then edit down the list to must-have items."

All in all, though, Flores says being a professional hauler hasn't changed much about her shopping habits. "I'm simply sharing what I would be shopping for and trying on anyway," she explains. That's why her videos are so relatable—they don't feel exaggerated or unrealistic. Instead, they offer a window into the world of our design partnerships from our avid fans and guests.

Stills from YouTuber Jessica Flores' Victoria Beckham for Target haul video, 2017

Altuzarra
2014

ALTUZARRA

A Real Day-to-Night Wardrobe with Joseph Altuzarra

Joseph Altuzarra launched his namesake label in New York in 2008, a time when a Barneys buyer would agree to sit on the floor of his parent's living room to survey his new creations. Since its conception, Altuzarra has been a leader in the luxury womenswear market (the designer cut his teeth as Riccardo Tisci's first assistant at Givenchy). Inspired by his international upbringing—in Paris, by a Chinese American mother and a French Basque father—Altuzarra has mastered the mix of French seduction and American sensibility; a combination that encourages the endless possibilities of womanhood. His clothes succeed in making sophistication sexy. Perhaps it's the eight years he spent studying ballet that informed his understanding of movement, flow, and the way fabrics move with ease around the body.

In 2014, the same year he was named Womenswear Designer of the Year at the CFDA awards, we invited Altuzarra to collaborate. His signature—staunch femininity and sensual textures—was expressed via snakeskin prints, structured trench coats and crimson pantsuits cast in velvet. Much of his 50-piece line had an after-dark sensibility, with belted waists and over-the-knee boots. Even with all its high-fashion styling, the line promised total functionality: dresses were designed to look like two separate pieces, sweaters were adorned with the same details as satin shirts and the hems of skirts skimmed the knee, adding total ease of movement.

Portrait of Joseph Altuzarra

Opposite: Campaign photographed by Peter Lindbergh, featuring model Eva Herzigová

ALTUZARRA

Toughness meets
sensuality with a slick,
over-the-knee boot

NO
PARKING

Proenza
Schouler
2007

Proenza Schouler's Benevolent Beauty

Lazaro Hernandez and Jack McCollough of Proenza Schouler, photographed by Djamilla Rosa Cochran, 2007

Opposite:
A selection of looks from the Proenza Schouler for Target collection

Lazaro Hernandez and Jack McCollough met at Parsons, where they were mentored by *Project Runway* maven Tim Gunn. They bonded quickly, and permanently—even today, they finish each other's sentences and rarely spend time apart. In 2002, the pair collaborated on a collection for their joint senior thesis, naming it Proenza Schouler, a combination of their mothers' maiden names. Barneys New York bought the entire line—a surprising coup for the young talents. From there, success followed rapidly. In 2004, the womenswear designers received the first ever CFDA Vogue Fashion Fund award; one of the highest industry honors, it came with a $400,000 prize for young designers to develop their brand. Hernandez and McCollough were instantly anointed by the fashion media as the bold new face of New York design. The "Proenza Schouler woman" felt like an immediately recognizable and appealing archetype: preppy and elegant, but not afraid to loosen up.

Three years later, in 2007, Hernandez and McCollough partnered with us for a collection that brought their designs to the masses. They delivered a striking line of resort wear, including silk jersey dresses, slinky cardigans with floral prints, sleek swimwear and bustier-top dresses in bright jewel tones—the latter, a label signature. Our collection was simultaneously carried at the high-concept Paris boutique Colette, making it the first time our clothes were sold outside of the US.

"I've worked with Proenza Schouler from the beginning," said Colette's Sarah Lerfel, speaking to the *Times*. They have always been very sure of their new silhouette, very chic—but not full of clichés, so that their clothes look fresh, strong and elegant." Hernandez and McCollough haven't slowed since. Though the clothes have always felt ahead of the curve, they've never sacrificed high-quality tailoring and attention to detail in order to get there. Two decades later, Proenza Schouler continues to define a particular brand of cutting-edge style, approachable and elevated.

PROENZA SCHOULER

KATE YOUNG
FOR TARGET

Kate Young
2013

EXIT

KATE YOUNG

Painting the Town Red (Carpet) with Kate Young

Kate Young is more than a stylist to the stars: she's a style star in her own right. Her career is every bit as dynamic as her clientele—she's counted Sienna Miller, Michelle Williams, Natalie Portman and Selena Gomez among her roster.

Getting her start at *Vogue* in the late 90s, where she served as Anna Wintour's assistant, Young cut her teeth in the editorial world, serving as the Fashion Editor at Large for *Interview* and lending her sartorial eye to publications like *i-D*, *Glamour*, and *InStyle*. It was her willingness to work hard from day one that led her to Hollywood, where she has since carved a unique space for herself as a celebrity stylist and creative consultant.

As a stylist, Young has a few golden rules. She never dresses clients in black—too boring—and for every red carpet appearance, she makes an entire inspiration binder, tailored to her star.

While it's the exact combination of these characteristics that drew our team to Young, a particular binder—brimming with classic movie references—ended up laying the foundation for our entire collection.

Inspired by Hollywood haute—be it Natalie Portman, who Young dressed in vintage Dior, or Dakota Johnson, who she outfitted in Hedi Slimane's Celine—her looks for us included ultra-feminine, strapless minis with ruffles and bows, and flowing gowns with daring back details. Kate Young for Target was a collection of party girl glam, priced to wear to proms and quinceañeras, even weddings. The launch party was themed around prom too, held at a gym at the Old Cathedral School in Lower Manhattan. At the door, every guest was presented with a tissue paper corsage, fashioned by artists that Young herself chose.

Kate Young, photographed by Eugene Gologursky, 2010

Opposite: The Kate Young for Target prom party launch event, photographed by Neil Rasmus

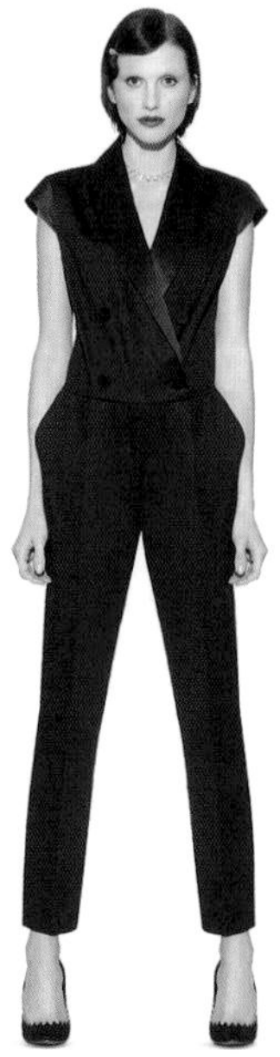
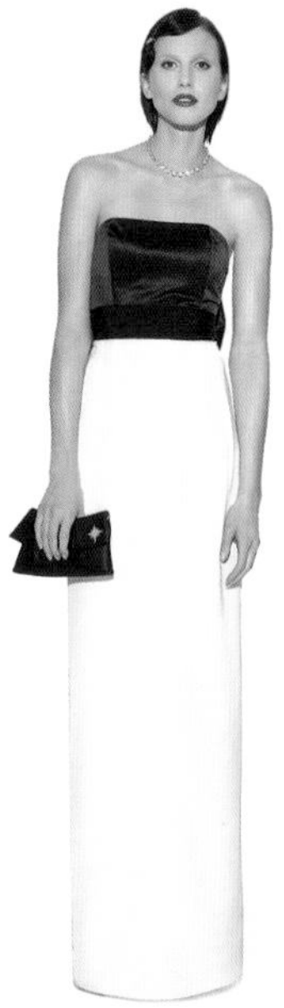

Opposite:
A selection of looks
from Kate Young for
Target collection

Neiman
Marcus
2012

Shock of the New: A Hi-Tech, Holiday Collection with Neiman Marcus

In 2012 Target partnered with Neiman Marcus for an audacious experiment—we tapped 24 of our favorite designers to craft us special one-off items. Each studio stretched beyond their comfort zone to provide guests with a holiday collection unlike any they'd seen before, using complex production techniques to elevate the everyday. In celebration, we donated $1 million to the CFDA Fashion Fund—helping young American designers find their footing.

Many designers who traditionally made clothes opted instead for playful toys or home goods. Joseph Altuzarra made a bar set that boasted intricate glassware. "It was made in the same factory Versace makes its drinkware in—the employee who used to run the factory came out of retirement to produce these," says Greg Van Bellinger, our Vice President of Product Design. "The glass features an interlocking diamond shape around the outside; to get it to fit perfectly we had to produce a custom algorithm and a 3D model."

The iconic fashion house Oscar de la Renta turned heads with a ceramic dog bowl, built using a high-tech molding technique. We partnered with the brand's head of design and our 3D designer to help visualize the complicated form. "They had a piece of lace that they wanted wrapped around a ceramic bowl. That was really intricate," said Kellie Rosen, who works on our design partnerships for the home. "Our vendor had never done anything like that before."

The ambitious, multi-designer project required a literal mad-dash of effort to complete. Van Bellinger recalls the team driving from studio to studio, negotiating between designers over who would get to make which product for Target. "Someone said, 'Well I want to do a bike,' but I'm like, 'We already promised a bike to Alice + Olivia!'" he recalls.

It was all worth it for results like Derek Lam's marvelous skateboard. Lam designed a board with laser-cut pattern grip tape, something that just might have been a world first. "We had numerous sessions with the world's biggest skateboard manufacturer on how to bring this thing to life," recalls Tim Kehoe, who worked on partnerships with Van Bellinger. In the end, the pair-up proved a smashing success, in which we came away inspired by the ingenuity of our partners. "It wasn't a financial transaction," remembers Kehoe, fondly. "It was a meeting of the minds."

Opposite:
Neiman Marcus for Target, featuring Karlie Kloss, photographed by Craig McDean

This exclusive collection featured 50 gorgeous gifts from 24 top designers

Best
Friends
CAROLINA HERRERA
CAROLINA HERRERA
CAROLINA HERRERA

Phillip Lim
2013

Phillip Lim's Lifelong Love Affair with Elegance

"It's kind of like dating," said Phillip Lim, when the *New York Times* asked him about the lead-up to his collection for us in 2013 (we'd actually approached him five years before). "Finally at this moment, we're like, OK, maybe we're both mature enough and our expectations are more realistic of what we want from each other."

For Lim, the anticipation had been building for, well, his whole life. His parents—a professional poker player and a seamstress—emigrated to the United States after fleeing the Cambodian Genocide. He grew up shopping for back-to-school essentials at Target.

Lim's love affair with fashion began in his youth, when he worked at an Orange County department store. He parlayed his interest in clothes into an internship with the enigmatic designer Katayone Adeli—who he discovered while unpacking boxes of merchandise at work. In 2005, the fresh-faced designer teamed up with his friend Wen Zhou to kick-start his eponymous line, 3.1 Phillip Lim. Its sense of easy, throw-on elegance quickly made waves, attracting a stable of celebrity fans including Kate Hudson, Scarlett Johansson and Keira Knightley.

In 2007, the influential Council of Fashion Designers of America gave Lim its award for Emerging Talent in Womenswear—an honor that's often indicated the start of a bright career.

When it finally came out, Lim's collection for us was a smash success. Divided into morning, noon and night wardrobes—ensuring around-the-clock relevance—many styles sold out within the first day. It included both mens' and womenswear; sweaters, pants and trench coats in neutral tones, plus high-impact graphic pieces with punchy, comic book graphics.

"I think my job is to express and provide clothing and products that actually capture time and are, at the same time, timeless," Lim told *The Cut*, speaking about our collection. "The whole idea of clothes is, let it be, and pick what's personal to you, what works for you, what you desire and I think that the rest, just let it fall into place."

You can sense what he means when you look at each garment; sophisticated without feeling stuffy, dressed up and down at once, equally suited for layering, or statement-makers on their own.

Portrait of Phillip Lim, by Jacob Sutton

Opposite:
3.1 Phillip Lim for Target, features a collection that can take you from a.m. to p.m.

8:45 AM
3.1 Phillip Lim
SEPTEMBER 15
IN SELECT STORES AND TARGET.COM
FOR A LIMITED TIME ONLY #PhillipLimForTarget

BOOM
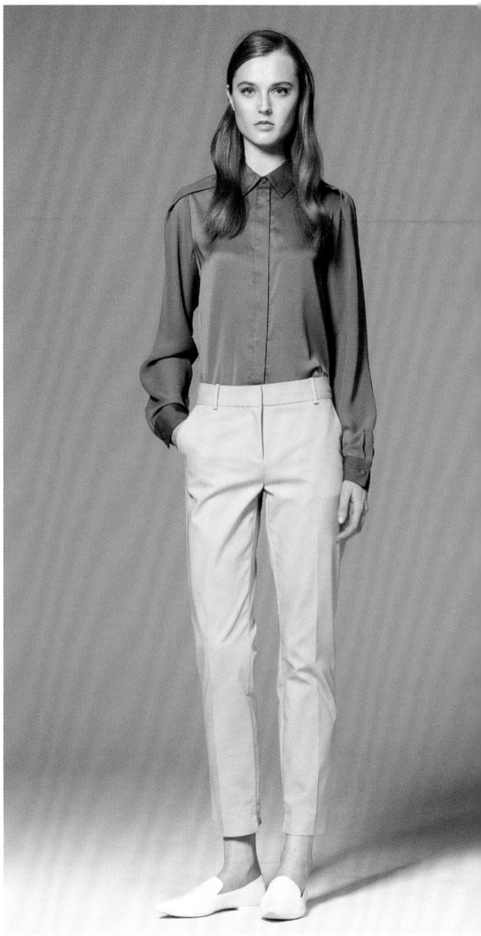

Phillip Lim

These graphic prints were borrowed from comics: Sin City and V for Vendetta

Zac Posen
2010

Zac Posen Knows What People Want (to Wear)

It's almost as if Zac Posen was born to be a designer. As a child growing up in a Jewish New York family, he used to steal yarmulkes—brimless caps, made from cloth—from the local synagogue and transform them into doll-sized ball dresses. At 16, he interned for designer Nicole Miller; at 21 he opened a makeshift studio in his parent's living room. Posen has an innate desire to inspire the way people get dressed, likely informed, in part, by his education at Central Saint Martins college of art and design in London.

Posen's inventiveness paid off. In 2000, a dress he designed for supermodel Naomi Campbell ended up in the hands of actress Paz de la Huerta. She was spotted wearing it to a party, then loaned it to a friend, who wore it to Kate Hudson's wedding. Call it fashion folklore, but this series of switches launched Posen's already promising career. Since then, his line has been praised for its craftsmanship and consideration of the female form.

In 2010, a year after debuting his futuristic, plexiglass-plated party wear in New York, we partnered with Posen to produce a collection reinterpreting his most iconic styles. A line of apparel that included outerwear and swim, Zac Posen for Target embodied the many ways contemporary women get dressed. From tuxedo suits to floor-length gowns (a first for Posen), the vibe was rock royalty meets Italian villa vacation—and no garment was spared his signature attention to detail.

Portrait of Zac Posen

Opposite: Campaign photographed by Ellen von Unwerth

A selection of looks from the 40-piece Zac Posen for Target collection

Opposite: Campaign photographed by Ellen von Unwerth

Jonathan
Saunders
2008

Art School Confidential: How Jonathan Saunders Made Fashion From Art

Glaswegian Jonathan Saunders is one of the foremost designers to break out of the UK over the past 20 years. In 2002, he started his namesake line, quickly drawing attention for its sleek tailoring, bright colors, and unusual prints. Often, you'd find nature seeping into his designs: a black pantsuit featuring beaded birds, a dress with fluttering fabric panels, like a flower. He'd go on to run it for 14 years, before accepting a role as creative director at Diane von Furstenberg.

It was at legendary London fashion school Central Saint Martins where Saunders first spread his wings. He recalled his shock upon first meeting his fellow students, decked out in their own designs. "I assumed everyone in the fashion industry looked like this," he told *1Granary*, joking that in comparison, "I looked like a tramp."

At school, Saunders found himself part of a group of brilliant young British designers. "Richard Nicoll was on the same course," he said. "Christopher Kane was in the year below, and Roksanda was in the year above." Like Kane, Saunders was drawn to loud, graphic prints, an interest he credits to an education that encouraged him to form "an opinion and a point of view."

Saunders' graduate collection earned him praise from the press and a prestigious Lancôme Color Design Award—plus consultancies with Phoebe Philo at Chloé, Christian Lacroix at Pucci, and Alexander McQueen. The latter hired him two days after he graduated. Saunders went on to design the famous Birds of Paradise print for McQueen's Spring 2003 ready-to-wear collection.

Over the rest of the 2000s, Saunders' brand continued turning heads, including ours. In 2008, we tapped him for a special line of womenswear inspired by artists Gustav Klimt, Jackson Pollock, and Mark Rothko. To that end, he created an intoxicating mix of red and blue dresses, wildly printed button-downs, and sleek turtle-necks—modeled in the lookbook by a young Hanne Gaby. "My collection for Target is refined with an edge," he said, adding that it "allows me to share my vision of individualism with women everywhere."

The stand-out piece—a magnetic, color-blocked tunic—is a painting you can wear. Saunders performed a magic trick, transforming patterns and colors from the avant-garde into a museum-worthy collection.

Jonathan Saunders, photographed by Christian MacDonald

Opposite: A selection of looks from the 40-piece Jonathan Saunders for Target collection

Erin
Fetherston
2007

Timeless: How Erin Fetherston Reshaped the Statement Bag

Statement bags are nothing new. In fact, they may be (nearly) as ancient as civilization itself. On top of a mountain in Southeast Turkey, there's a temple complex called Göbekli Tepe, which archaeologists believe dates back to 11,000 BCE. One pillar is adorned with carvings of what appear to be handbags. Some experts believe the bags represent the temple, a place where the divine and physical worlds come together. How's *that* for a statement?

A lot of things changed between the Göbekli Tepe's construction and the dawn of online shopping, but one thing stayed basically the same—we hunt for meaningful objects to carry around. Bags are the perfect totem: an item that represents who you are (and what you love) to the world, with a neat handle attached. Look no further than the mania that surrounds "it" bags—from the Fendi Baguette to the Yves Saint Laurent Muse, each inspires a quasi-religious devotion.

The internet is crawling with handbag-obsessed shoppers. In 2007, these connoisseurs turned their attention to American designer Erin Fetherston's line for us, finding a large, playful, heart-shaped handbag nestled among her mod-inspired dresses, tulle skirts, and Peter Pan-collar coats. The bright red bag became a defining moment for Fetherston, who'd debuted her brand of whimsical womenswear only two years prior at Fashion Week in Paris. Teaming up with Target exposed her vision to people all over America, who fell in love with her sweet shapes and silhouettes.

And at the same time, a new, more accessible "it" bag was born: one with an extra dose of pre-emoji graphic charm. Resembling a satiny red box of Valentine's Day chocolates—and spotted on Zooey Deschanel and in an episode of *Gossip Girl*—the statement heart bag sold out almost immediately, becoming one of the 2000s-era's most coveted carryalls.

Erin Fetherston, photographed by Patrick McMullan, 2017

Opposite: Heart bag by Erin Fetherston for Target

EXPECT MORE. PAY LESS.
la fête
erin
GO
International Flights of Fashion℠
Available at most stores and at Target.com/go

Silk charmeuse dress 59.99
Peter Pan-collar dress 49.99
Heart handbag 29.99
fetherston™

Many of them cut their teeth in downtown Manhattan—a jumbled, dizzying mecca for outsiders with something to prove. There was visionary punk kid Stephen Sprouse from Ohio, who quickly made his way into Andy Warhol's circle. There was Detroit-born Anna Sui, who launched her label in her living room. Some came from abroad—think defiant Frenchman Jean Paul Gaultier or London's Alexander McQueen—but they shared the anything-goes ethos. These are the rule breakers and culture shapers who became fashion icons—and shared their vision with America through Target.

Alexander McQueen
2009

Anna Sui
2009

Fiorucci
2005

Jean Paul Gaultier
2010

Stephen Burrows
2010

Rodarte
2009

Stephen Sprouse
2002

Mavericks

TRUTH

Alexander
McQueen
2009

Love looks not
with the eyes,
But with the

The Rock 'n' Roll, Stageworthy Vision of Alexander McQueen

Alexander McQueen, born Lee Alexander, decided he was going to be a designer at the ripe old age of 16. The son of a London taxi driver, he left school that year to serve as a tailor's apprentice on Savile Row, working with theatrical costumers. He was then accepted into Central Saint Martins, where hyper-influential stylist—and eccentric aristocrat—Isabella Blow bought his entire grad collection for £5,000. Blow became his longtime mentor, suggesting he drop Lee professionally and use his middle name instead.

It wasn't long before McQueen brought his renegade breed of gothic romance to his own label—and later, the house of Givenchy. With a taste for the surreal and sublime, McQueen made every Fashion Week a theatrical spectacle—setting runways on fire, drenching models in rain, and spray-painting dresses with mechanized robotic arms. (His earliest collections included samples of his own hair sewn into the label.) A master provocateur, his designs stitched together contemporary womanhood, whimsical fantasy, and centuries of British history with a generous dose of mischief. McQueen's collection for us is as iconic as any, drawing inspiration from the late designer's muse: the ever-youthful, platinum-haired British rocker Liela Moss. In it, classic prom dresses, tuxedo jackets, and matching shorts are sharper—often with asymmetrical cuts—and there are electric shocks of pink and blue alongside punky, sharp-toothed hardware. Britannia rock 'n' roll comes to America.

Isabella Blow in Alexander McQueen, photographed by Dave Benett, 1995

Opposite: Alexander McQueen, photographed by Ann Ray

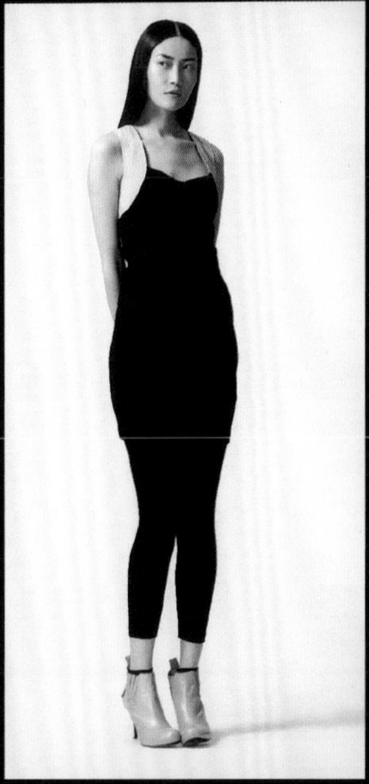

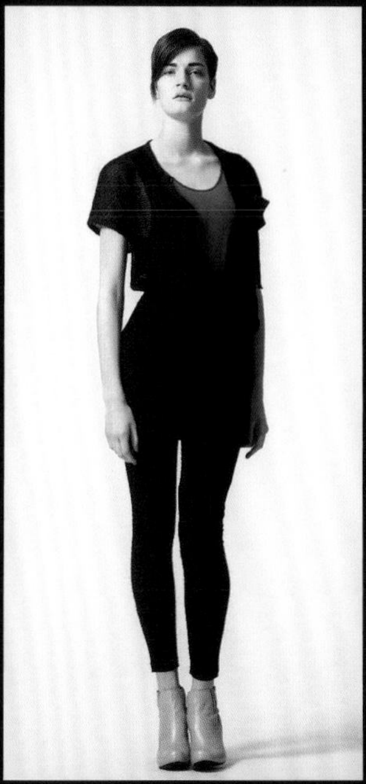

A selection of images from the 30-piece McQ Alexander McQueen for Target collection

AARON DOUGLAS
COSTUME & FASHION

In Conversation with Blythe Doll Customizer Phillip Noel

Interview by Laura Bannister
Photography by Vincent Dilio

Before Alexander McQueen's rocker collection appeared in stores—or on the bodies of real people—there were the dolls, splashed across billboards. Specifically, Blythe dolls customized by the British designer himself: all big, glassy, dinner-plate eyes, supersized heads, and cute-creepy demeanor, each outfitted in mini versions of his line. Not only did the fashion world notice—it's not every day a gang of giant dolls tease a collection drop—but a global community of toy collectors, for whom the ultra-rare doll is an infatuation.

Inspired by Margaret Keane's paintings from the 60s, with their otherworldly, wide-eyed girls, Blythe was only sold in the US for the year of 1972—marketed as a fashion doll—before being discontinued. Since then, copycats and other distributors have popped up, and the once-unpopular Blythe has become a phenomenon, a big-headed optical illusion made real. For the creatively minded, like the late McQueen, their surreal forms and cartoonish features are a pleasurable challenge: Blythe's faces can be reworked, new personalities invented, and tiny outfits crafted to their forms. One such customizer is Phillip Noel, a New York fashion designer with a DIY Blythe fixation. Over email, we discussed what McQueen's Blythe moment meant, and dipped our toes into the valley of the dolls.

LAURA BANNISTER Can you tell me a little about yourself?
PHILLIP NOEL I've been into art since I was a child, was always drawing something, always making something, even my own toys. Always had a doll obsession. I went to school for fashion at Parsons in New York. I get up and go to my design job each day, then come and work on [Blythes]. The dolls are what feed my creativity—I don't have to answer to anyone when creating them. I'm constantly looking at dolls, makeup, fashion, and nature for inspiration.

LB This is a broad question, but, as a fellow designer, what does McQueen mean to you?
PN McQueen has always been one of my undeniable favorites. He created this beautiful world where fashion met fantasy, larger-than-life clothes that felt otherworldly and [his shows] were cinematic. What I loved about him was his ability to take a theme and really develop it without it being cheesy or anything people had seen before. Every runway show told an entire story, down to the way the models walked. One of my favorite moments was Spring 2010, where models slinked down the runway slowly because their shoes were almost too large and heavy, but it felt so right.

McQueen has always been one of my undeniable favorites. He created this beautiful world where fashion met fantasy.

LB As you know, McQueen made a series of custom Blythe dolls for Target. Have you ever seen them in the flesh?
PN I remember when the ads came out. It was a big deal. But I didn't find out until later that McQueen himself customized the dolls. At this point, I only owned one myself—not a customized doll, but what we call a "stock" doll—or "as is"—sold by Takara and Hasbro. I'm not surprised McQueen liked Blythe, there is this edgy and at times dark feel to her. That was in his own work as well.

LB What did you think of Target featuring this niche product in a big way?
PN I loved them being used in the ads. They're so interesting to photograph—she really makes for the perfect model and Target and McQueen both saw that. I think Target allowed McQueen to be true to his eerie style in choosing to feature Blythe. I was also excited more people would know what I was talking about when I mentioned her.

LB What drew you to acquiring—and customizing—Blythe dolls too?
PN It was one of those strange things where I saw Blythe and immediately was intrigued. She was this mix of cute and weird—some may say creepy. Eleven years later, and I think she looks as normal as a person on the street. Her head isn't so huge to me anymore, I've grown to know and adore her. I think I was drawn to customizing her because she's so unique and iconic, but a great base for an artist to create their own character. I've customized other dolls but Blythe is by far my favorite. She has so much personality and attitude. I love that she doesn't have to be smiling either, she can actually look quite melancholy. Blythe has a large head that lends itself to customization, you get a much bigger canvas to work on than, say, a Barbie, [though] she's about the same height. I've never attempted to carve on a vinyl doll—Blythe is one of the few with a hard-plastic head. Like I said, there are so many elements to her: she gets four pairs of eyes that are revealed each time you pull a string, and you can paint and customize them. You can give her entirely new hair. You can plop her head on a different body if you want. And, of course, there's the clothes—she was meant to be a fashion doll and that's a big part of collecting and customizing.

LB Is there any correlation between your work as a designer and the garments you create for the dolls?
PN Definitely. I like to dress them in what I want to see people wearing. If I design differently for her it's because you can go further, because she's just a doll. I think my whole thing was dressing them as I would design clothes. I think I make sexier clothes for my dolls than most customizers and more fashion focused than focused on being "cute," or clothes that the average person would relate to. She's a doll—for me, I like her to represent a fantasy, not reality. For me, customizing and creating a doll is another extension of me as an artist and designer, so I try to keep true to myself.

LB Can you explain the customization process?
PN I usually spend a few hours at a time carving and modifying her face—probably two to three hours over [a few] days. And when I'm happy with her look, I sand her until she's smooth and ready to paint. I mostly carve and modify her face using a curved X-Acto, sandpaper, and different sanding files. As for painting and coloring, I use crushed pastels (they become like makeup), acrylics, pearl, and metallic pigments and a whole lot of sealant. I've done hair re-roots out of fibers like mohair or alpaca. Often I end up giving their original hair a wash and nice cut. There is almost nothing that can't be customized on this doll—there's always a way you can take them to a new level. When they're finished, they really are a piece of art.

LB You mentioned the McQ McQueen for Target dolls were a surprisingly diverse group. Can you expand on the significance of featuring McQueen-customized girls with different skin tonalities?
PN I love that they used Blythe the same way they would use real life models—Target is always diverse and meant to reach everyone. There isn't a wide range of Blythe skin tones manufactured today, certainly not on the original dolls from the 70s. The ability to create a diversity is one of my favorite aspects of customization ... I think the realistic and diverse group of dolls helped keep the campaign down to earth and humanize the dolls in a way.

This and previous spread: Phillip Noel in his apartment, surrounded by his Blythe Dolls and inspiration boards

Anna Sui
2009

EP:113
B304
8 N
GOSSIP GIRL
J. MILLER TOBIN
3/14/08

Harnessing the Energy of NY Cool Girls with Anna Sui

To understand the magic of our *Gossip Girl*-inspired line with Anna Sui, you need to know how the Illinois native became NYC's go-to master of escapism: you can be absolutely anyone in her clothes—a punk, a schoolgirl, an androgynous vision, a super-modern Victorian.

As a four-year-old growing up in Detroit, Sui had a vision of her adult life as a designer—one she guesses she borrowed from some television show. "I always had it in mind that a designer had beautiful fabrics around her and a big sketchbook, and would drape cloth around a mannequin, and go out to lunch," she says. "It seemed like a very glamorous life." Sui began following her mother to fabric shops, repurposing her sewing scraps as clothes for Barbies, then herself.

Fast-forward to downtown Manhattan in 1992, and Sui was opening her very first store, having fallen in with SoHo's resident cool crowd—Marc Jacobs, Todd Oldham and Steven Meisel—and embraced their go-getter spirit. Entered through an elaborate wardrobe door (a nod to the children's classic *The Lion, The Witch and The Wardrobe*) it featured bright red floorboards, purple walls, and antique furniture rails packed with offbeat, gloriously mishmash styles. Oh—and everyone was there. At least, it felt like it.

Her first runway shows had the same hyped-up energy and mish-mash, house party aesthetic: Naomi Campbell and Linda Evangelista danced down her runways in feathers, bows, rhinestones, and polka-dots. It was pink lip gloss meets black lip liner. It was icons, outfitted by Sui. And so it seemed perfect that, in 2009, at the height of *Gossip Girl* mania—the TV show spotlighting wealthy Manhattan teens—Sui would turn the show's spirit into a Target collection about women in Manhattan, expressing themselves however they pleased.

Separated into four groups, each one inspired by a persona of the show's four characters, our line together uses the show's narrative to tell a story, Sui style. There's mixed prints (Vanessa), deep cuts (Jenny), girly bows (Blair), and a few adventurous details (Serena). We launched it with a pop-up shop party, rejigging a SoHo space into an Upper East Side mansion. The star-studded guest list included the entire cast of the show.

Anna Sui photographed by Kwaku Alston

Opposite: On the set of *Gossip Girl*, the show that inspired Anna Sui's Target collection, photographed by James Devaney, 2008

At the time of the collaboration, I had recently traveled through China and was surprised the Chinese girls I met were totally obsessed with *Gossip Girl*—they watched it religiously online. Everyone was asking me to tell them details about the show and especially about the various New York neighborhoods where the characters live—the Upper East Side, the East Village, Williamsburg. The spirit of the collection was meant to represent the style of the show's characters. I think that *Gossip Girl* was very influential on how girls dressed all over the world!

Anna Sui

Sui's 47-piece collection included one-of-a-kind totes made from vinyl Target billboards displayed in Times Square. The bag became a campaign image, with illustrations by artist Laurie Rosenwald

Opposite: Stills from the Anna Sui for Target TV commercial

FIOR

Fiorucci
2005
UCCI®

Dancing in the Daytime: Why Artists Flock to Fiorucci

Fiorucci, once fondly referred to as "daytime Studio 54," opened its first American emporium in 1976 on New York's East 59th Street. The Italian shop quickly became the nucleus of cool, around which the famous and fascinating orbited—thousands of them on any given Saturday. The glitter-strewn store was where a young Marc Jacobs first met designer Calvin Klein. It was where silver-screen icon Lauren Bacall discovered sportswear, where Cher spent $1,000 on an assortment of "gilt and glorious trash," and where Madonna's brother once punched a timecard as an employee. (Madonna herself performed at Studio 54 for the 15th anniversary party of the Fiorucci label, ahead of the release of "Like a Virgin.") As Priscilla Tucker wrote in the March 1977 issue of *New York Magazine*: "All it took this year to achieve instant chic, day or night, at the slickest New York party or the trashiest, was a pair of $110 gold cowboy boots from Fiorucci."

"Went to Fiorucci and it's so much fun there," Warhol wrote in 1983 in *The Andy Warhol Diaries*. "It's everything I've always wanted, all plastic." The Pope of Pop Art was a fixture at Fiorucci, often signing copies of *Interview* magazine with author Truman Capote in the windows. His friendship with founder Elio Fiorucci lasted until Warhol's death in 1987.

But so much of Fiorucci's fabulousness was in the clothes they made—vinyl trousers, angel-stamped denim, and T-shirts soaked with nostalgia. Its founder told *New York Magazine* back in 1977 that "it's no longer in fashion to be in fashion … The streets should be a panorama of effortless surprises." When we approached the riotous brand to collaborate and share that anything-goes ethos with Americans everywhere, the result was poptastic prints, low-slung jeans, and more-is-more 80s brashness mixed with a heavy dose of humor. It was bright, bold, and covered in kisses, ready for a new generation to party in.

Elio Fiorucci, photographed by Mondadori Portfolio, 1965

Opposite: A punk fashion show at the Fiorucci store in Beverly Hills, photographed by George Rose, 1979

STYLE INVASION!!
Fiorucci fever takes over Target!!
FIORUCCI
...the Italian label that invented designer jeans and pop art as fashion
Fiorucci rhymes with smoochie
FIORUCCI®
available in stores and at Target.com in early december
Trench coat 39.99
Cowgirl tee 12.99
Gingham shirt 24.99
Cuffed crop jeans 39.99
Cherub tote 29.99

Zip hooded sweater 24.99
Fiorucci tee 12.99
Zip-pocket jeans 39.99
Rainbow belt 12.99
Denim jacket 49.99
Zip jacket 29.99
Embroidered crop pants 39.99
Studded tank 14.99
a quick kiss of fashion
get it now!!
send a smoochie, go to:
www.sendasmoochie.com

STYLE INVASION!!
Fiorucci fashion fever takes over Target!!
This winter Target heats things up with the electric energy of Fiorucci® Available for a limited time, the Fiorucci brand will include retro-inspired screened tees, denim, miniskirts, cargo pants, handbags and more. The nostalgic brand reflects a playful and lively spirit and is available exclusively at Target stores from December 2005 through January 2006.
All images are included on disc.
FIORUCCI
39.99
39.99
For More Information Contact:
Genna Blackman
LaForce + Stevens
Phone: 212.242.9353, ext. 146
E-mail: genna@laforce-stevens.com

From a behind-the-scenes perspective, the most thrilling thing was working out how to get stores excited before launch day. I had a vintage Fiorucci tin, and in one of our meetings I brought it up. We developed it, and made Fiorucci T-shirts with sequined, sparkling lips. We rolled them up in the tins, along with the lookbook and instructions on how to merchandise the collection. It was sent to stores a month ahead to build hype. It was the first time we'd done anything like that before.

Wendy Santana, long-term design partnerships collaborator

Fiorucci for Target press images, including a pop-out CD-ROM

Jean Paul
Gaultier
2010

Pop for the People with Jean Paul Gaultier

French revolutionary Jean Paul Gaultier is often dubbed fashion's "enfant terrible" for his shrewd shock tactics—but it's his obsession with pop icons we wanted to share with guests. Referencing his most notorious pieces for pop queens like Madonna, our collaboration danced across punk, hip-hop, Hollywood glamour, and everything in between. There were silky tops and mesh gloves shorn off above the palm, classic leather bikers, and Breton stripes. In short, there were pop-identities for myriad women to embody, fusing French and all-American aesthetics. In an interview with *Dazed*, the designer once said his shows celebrated the same diversity: "I don't want to have just one specific image of a woman in my shows, I want to present what really exists."

When he was a kid, the enterprising Gaultier betrayed his own star quality, posting sketches to his fashion heroes in the hopes of gaining their attention. On his 18th birthday, the move paid off, when he was hired as an assistant to avant-garde designer Pierre Cardin. (The Frenchman told a young Gaultier to reach for the moon, or at least design for women who were headed there.)

Six years later, Gaultier released his first solo collection—and was quickly praised for his razor-sharp tailoring, unconventional runway casting, and undergarments reframed as outerwear. (There was the pink cone corset bra, custom-made for Madonna's "Blonde Ambition" tour, and other lingerie was spun from wire cages and mountains of purple velour.) Gaultier then followed in Martin Margiela's footsteps, with a stint as the creative director of Hermès. When his tenure at Hermès was up, we tapped him for Target—inspired by his ability to generate fantasies in an instant—and the legendary line was born.

Jean Paul Gaultier, photographed by Ian Cook, 1990

Opposite: Gaultier models at Paris Fashion Week, photographed by PL Gould, circa 1979

Melange TINA TURNER
BEYONCE SHAKIRA
+ GLAM
Creoles
Foulard
Bijoux Sautoi
Robe Bustier
plissée
Bracelets
Mitai
Resi
résilles coupées
BEYONCE

chemise Blanche
Veste Raye
Blouse ou
Blanche
robe qui
dépasse du Kilt
Kilt
raye
chaussett
BRITNEY

Gaultier was so warm and sharing to staff. He was a true gentleman. For every designer, there's one challenge I love to take on as my own—this one was a fabric Gaultier referred to as "Cloque." You can imagine him saying it in his beautiful French accent. It sounded like a dessert. I couldn't wait to develop the material. We finally nailed it. He was very pleased with the outcome.

Wendy Santana, long-term design partnerships collaborator

A look from Jean Paul Gaultier for Target collection

Opposite: Campaign image for Jean Paul Gaultier for Target collection, 2010

Previous spread: Original sketches by Jean Paul Gaultier for his Target collection

Stephen
Burrows
2010

The Soulful World of Stephen Burrows, Brimming with Disco-era Classics

Widely recognized as the first African American designer to gain international prominence—and the first man to really make fashion dance—mambo-lover Stephen Burrows dressed everyone from disco divas to Hollywood stars. (His shimmering gold chainmail dress for Farrah Fawcett is the stuff of Oscars legend.) Having graduated from New York's Fashion Institute of Technology in 1966, Burrows' arrival in the fashion world in the early 70s gave rise to a number of prominent African-American runway models, including supermodel Pat Cleveland. In 1972, he catapulted Black American excellence to global acclaim by competing in the "Battle of Versailles," a face-off in Paris pitting five US designers—including Burrows, Halston, and Oscar de la Renta—versus their French counterparts—like Yves Saint Laurent and Hubert Givenchy. Even then it was clear Burrows was a master of movement.

His dance-floor-ready designs felt fun and spontaneous because they were: he'd stretch edges, cut at all angles, and drape as he went, instead of working to traditional patterns.

A longtime resident of Harlem, Burrows has maintained the neighborhood's colorful legacy—his designs still feature celebratory, high-energy hues. And he stayed true to his love of the local for his 10-piece Target collaboration, which launched at the opening of our first Harlem store. 5% of profits were donated to the library of the Young Women's Leadership School in East Harlem. Though he made his mark on 60s and 70s fashion with swinging dresses in swirling primary shades, Burrows' color-blocked, mod-ish Target designs still hum with futuristic cool.

Stephen Burrows photographed by Karl Prouse, 2006

Opposite: Bethann Hardison, Stephen Burrows, and friends, photographed by Dustin Pittman, 1979

In Conversation with Stephen Burrows

Interview by Bethann Hardison

For Stephen Burrows and Bethann Hardison, the 70s were exactly as glamorous as one might imagine—the black-and-white imagery that floods the internet is proof. During that decade, Burrows was everywhere: his slinky, body-clinging, head-turning silhouettes a staple of New York's club scene, with seams that darted along the body at odd angles, deliberately uneven hems, and unlikely fusings of materials. From parties at Studio 54 to fashion shows in Paris, the designer and model ran with some of the industry's most iconic characters. Hardison was Burrows' showroom model turned muse—and later, a leader in providing advocacy and support for African American models, and *Vogue Italia*'s Editor at Large. Here, the pair reflect on their early days in New York and the designer's rise to fashion stardom, and his instinctive, carefree approach to design, which seeps into his brightly-colored line for us.

BETHANN HARDISON We first met at Henri Bendel's [the department store on 57th Street], before I was hired to be your showroom model, and now we have this long history.
STEPHEN BURROWS We love each other.

BH I have one photograph from when we went to *Tommy* (*Editor's Note*: the 1975 film based on a rock opera album by The Who), that was at the time we were hanging out at Studio 54 together. Do you remember going to the White House? You were invited and you took me along.
SB Yes! I danced with Betty Ford.

BH And I danced with the President. He came over and asked me to dance—I died. And Versailles was the year before that. It was bigger than anything, but we didn't think of it like that then. (*Editor's Note*: In 1973, five American fashion designers, including Oscar de la Renta, Anne Klein and Stephen Burrows, gathered at the Palace of Versailles to show against five French designers. It was an iconic, star-studded night marking a new era in American fashion.)
SB It was exciting that it was going to be in Paris—it was a benefit show. But I was lucky because I got all my girls.

BH You were making that signature dress; it was your tribute to couture. And then 30 years later, The Metropolitan Museum of Art gave [you] a citation about it. [Versailles has] had two documentaries, one book, and now HBO is going to do a feature film. Can you talk about your main muse [from that time]?

I didn't see any limitation in mixing the colors together—I did it with free abandon.

SB My muse was Pat Cleveland. She embodied my every woman. I could imagine her [dressed] in anything and it inspired me. Her whole being, her whole personality was something that I was akin to.

BH She's completely opposite to you in personality.
SB She's amazing in that way. All the [models] that were my favorites have their own strong personality. And they showed it on the runway, which is what made them so interesting. It was the way they moved, their whole movement.

BH Could you talk about your relationship with Target for the opening of the Harlem store?
SB It was great working with Target. We gave them the sketches, and a month later we had the samples, and it looked like they just took the sketch and turned it into the garment. It was great. It was such an easy effort to get to the stage that they did in one month.

BH And then we got the opportunity to do the exhibit at the Museum of the City of New York (*Editor's note: Stephen Burrows: When Fashion Danced* was staged in 2013, and sponsored by Target. It was the designer's first major retrospective). I was already working as a consultant to Target, and I wanted a museum that would see the worth in it and want to be involved. [The City Museum] was closer to where you lived, and the curator had always admired what you did. So it was perfect. They said yes right away, it was just a matter of raising funds. It was a wonderful thing to be able to go to Target and ask them to consider helping us.
SB Yeah, they did a great job.

BH I was really happy about that union [with Target]. So we had the event; the party which was exceptional. People flew in from different places, Roz [Rubenstein], one of your original partners from O Boutique, was there. How did you meet?
SB I met Rozzie when I went to school at FIT, and I met Bobby out on Fire Island. [Rozzie] got me my first gig doing clothes for [60s pop rock group] Jay and the Americans, who were friends of hers. I was making clothes for my friends, they all wanted the clothes I was wearing. One of my customers was this photographer named Sante Philano, and one of his friends that liked the clothes was this artist named Jimmie Vargas, and he wanted to open a bazaar with art and my clothes. When we formed O Boutique in 1968, we got Rozzie to come, and Bobby handled all of the menswear.

BH Wow, and that was across the street from the famous—
SB Max's Kansas City. We had a little factory in the basement of our store, everything I made for myself ended up in the collection. We did fashion shows in the window which got a lot of attention, and the clothes started taking over the art, but Jimmie didn't have the money to finance the clothing part, so O Boutique closed a year later. Then I went to Bendel's, and the whole group came: Rozzie, Bobby, Hector, my assistant.

BH And of course you became a sensation at Bendel's. Everyone respected you because you were so unique. [Which makes me ask] how you move from idea to garment?
SB Everything is done through sketching. I take pride in it coming out looking exactly like the sketch and that can be difficult to do. In the beginning, I wanted everything to be tight. I liked colorful things. I didn't see any limitation in mixing the colors together—I did it with free abandon. I was able to make things different because we figured out a way in the cutting process that made it so it came out random. That was my design theory at the time: just to do everything they said couldn't be done, like the idea of stripes needing to match. I said, "No they don't," and went on to do a collection that had stripes that didn't match.

BH You used certain industrial stitching, right?
SB When I was eight years old, I fell in love with the zigzag stitch on my grandmothers sewing machine. I wanted to make a dress for my girlfriend who lived upstairs, for her doll. I zigzagged the devil out of this little dress. The stitch was on the outside and it was in red and it was something I carried through great success in the beginning. And there was no lining. I couldn't understand why [other designers] would line a knit dress.

BH Back in those days, that was tradition. You came along as a maverick and did things so differently. A lot of students today design through computers. If you were to [start out] today, would you do it the same way?
SB Aesthetically, I'm just not familiar with the tech part, so I would need the technical assistance to do it today, and with pattern-making done by a computer, you risk it not coming out right. I mean, you do that with everything, but this way, you may have to make the thing three or four times before they get it right, which didn't happen before. I just find it easier to do it [the old] way.

BH Yeah. You're a person who really likes to work with the materials in person. As you work with it, you develop it.
SB That's true. It's how I always did it.

Opposite: Models, including Stephen Burrows' muse, Pat Cleveland, lift the designer above their heads in a 1977 issue of *Vogue*. Photographed by Oliviero Toscano

Rodarte
2009

The Rodarte sisters invited teen fashion blogger Tavi Gevinson to preview their Target collaboration; she was especially taken with a golden lace sweater.

Cinema Sisters: Bringing Rodarte's Hollywood Glamour to America

Rarely does a label evoke a complete narrative and captivating storytelling, season after season, unless you're talking about Rodarte. Helmed by sisters Kate and Laura Mulleavy, and headquartered in Los Angeles, the label is no stranger to Hollywood. From the explicit *Star Wars* detailing (read: dresses printed with Yoda and C-3PO) for Fall/Winter 2014, and the theatrical dry ice poison cloud hovering atop the runway for a *Mad Max*/Tim Burton-influenced Spring/Summer 2010, to their costume designs for *Black Swan*—the Mulleavy sisters tend to embrace high drama.

In fact, their cinematic inclinations were evident as far back as 2009, when we connected with the sisters for a line of ethereal womenswear. Case in point: a striped dress printed with a rib cage, recalling the skeletal rabbit from the 2001 film *Donnie Darko*. Then there's the sky blue dress, which exudes the same haunted preppy innocence as Kirsten Dunst's star-making role in the *Virgin Suicides*. The Rodarte woman plays the lead role in her own romantic narrative.

"What you'll notice is an amazing eye for detail," said Senior Director of Communications at Target, Joshua Thomas, in an interview with *WWD*. "It's very feminine, yet very modern. The collection incorporates a rich mix of patterns and fabrications and everything from sequins and bows to faux fur."

After years of creating clothes that evoked film romance, Rodarte surprised everyone again in 2017 when they released the trailer for their first feature length film, *Woodshock*, starring Dunst. "They are like nothing I've ever seen before, and there is such a story behind each collection," Dunst told *The Hollywood Reporter*. "I knew it would be a seamless transition into film." In one scene, Dunst levitates up through the forest, lifted by a harness high into the trees, where she enjoys a view otherwise reserved for birds. *Woodshock* and the Mulleavys' clothes both provide flights of fancy, inviting the women who love them to soar.

Kate and Laura Mulleavy, photographed by Autumn DeWilde

Opposite: Stills from Rodarte for Target TV commercial, featuring Tavi Gevinson, 2009

Previous and following spread: Campaign and press images photographed by Autumn DeWilde

Music is in Rodarte's DNA: after college, Kate sold off records in order to raise money for the first collection.

Stephen
Sprouse
2002

The Duke of Day-Glo, Stephen Sprouse, Takes America

"The Target collection came at a very exciting time for Stephen," recalls the designer's brother Brad. "His graffiti had really taken off, as had his work with neon colors. He was also very excited with the times we were living in: MTV, advancing technology, the internet. He loved that a kid in Indiana or Iowa now had the same access to fashion, music, and art as kids in New York City and Los Angeles."

Fans got their hands on a slice of Sprouse back in 2002, when the Indiana-born tastemaker debuted a red, white and blue Americana-themed collection with us, punctuated with his signature graffiti-scrawl type. He made it all in Minneapolis, at Target HQ, where he was known to work through the night, making art and music on the side.

"He was a creative genius," remembers Minda Gralnek, our former Vice President Creative Director. She was in charge of meeting with him in the evenings at his temporary art studio in Minneapolis to discuss products. She often brought her eleven-year-old daughter, Lila. The ever-generous Sprouse bonded with Lila—even asking for her creative advice as he worked. Once, in a meeting where he and Target executives were deciding between different options for a T-shirt, Gralnek remembers he turned to her and said, "Let's call Lila."

You can still find rare pieces online, like the reversible cotton bucket hat—emblazoned SPROUSE—that emerges intermittently on Grailed, its exterior dotted with shapes plucked straight from the US flag. It crystallized a style he'd pioneered for decades, inspired by the underground club scene of downtown New York. It fused an anarchic, DIY sensibility with all-American pedigree.

As an artistically inclined child, he was helped with an introduction to Norman Norell by his dad, and through that, he became an apprentice to Bill Blass at age 14. He later went to work with Halston, the 70s icon who catered to uptown doyennes and Studio 54 types, like Liza Minnelli and Marisa Berenson. He was loved by Blondie—Deborah Harry wore a strappy Sprouse dress covered in TV scan lines for a music video—and known for always carrying a pen, scribbling ideas everywhere. His clothing may have been made of space-age fabrics and in shades of neon (he actually collaborated with NASA on more than one occasion), but his Day-Glo fabrics were crafted by Agnona, a cashmere label from Italy.

Sprouse was a devoted friend and fan of Andy Warhol, and Warhol's approach to art and celebrity—borrowing from American iconography, with his own twist—was a method Sprouse used too. It's little wonder fellow club kid Marc Jacobs tapped Sprouse's brilliant, bright lettering to remake Louis Vuitton, stamping it all over the luxury brand's monogram in the 2000s, bringing the untouchable back to earth.

Stephen Sprouse and Andy Warhol, photographed by Martin Burgoyne

Opposite: Deborah Harry, photographed by Brian Aris

This pop-graffiti skateboard was among Sprouse's most popular Target pieces. According to the New York Times*, Chloë Sevigny even bought or*

TARGET® PRESENTS
AMERICALAND:
DESIGNS BY
STEPHEN SPROUSE.
AVAILABLE FOR A LIMITED TIME
AT TARGET STORES AND TARGET.COM.
SPROU
2002

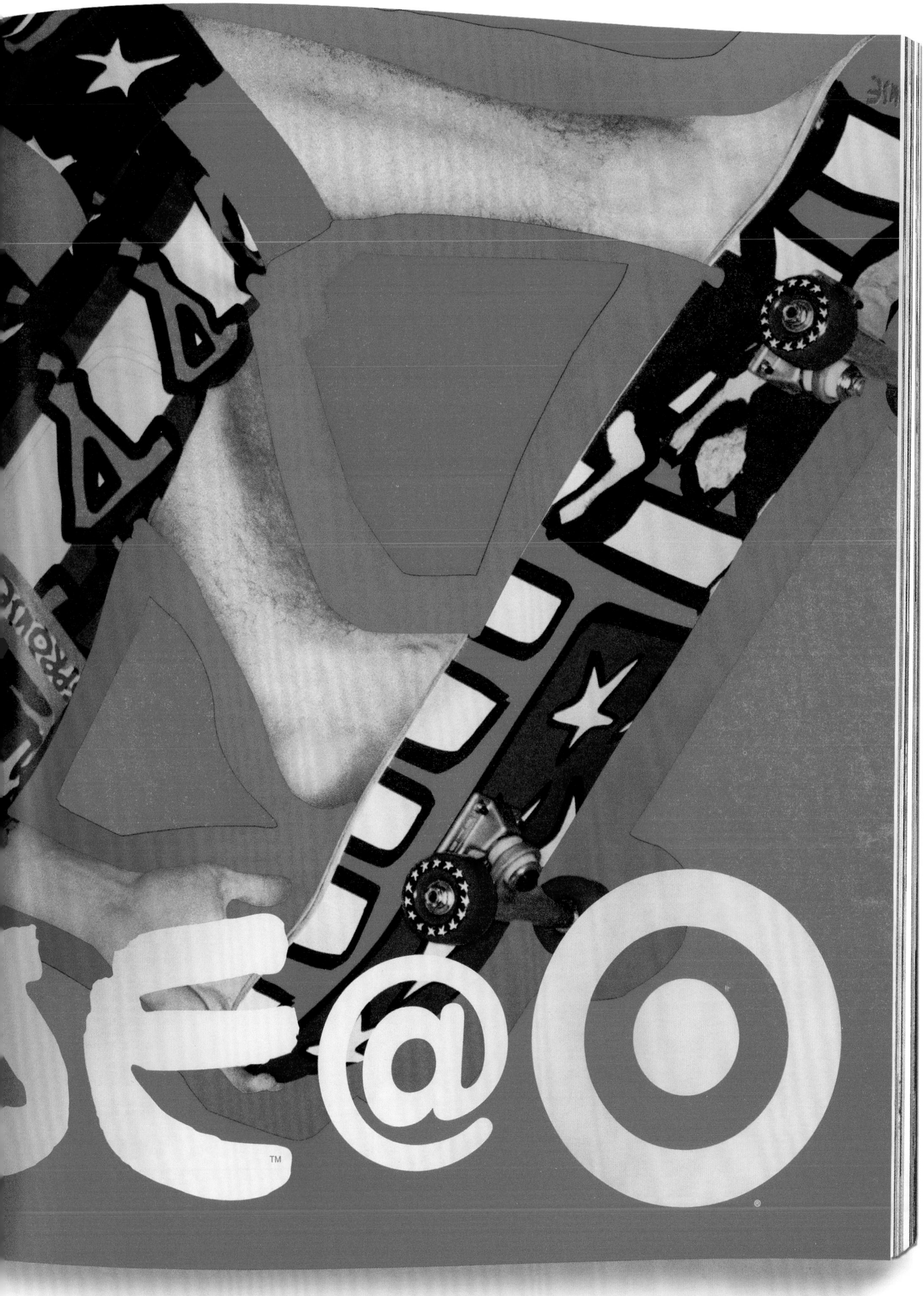

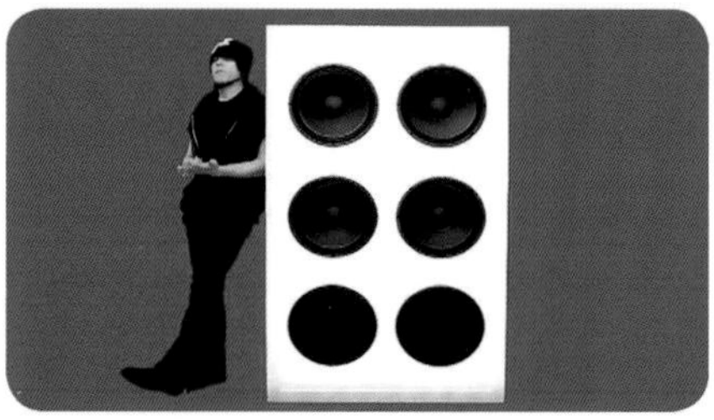

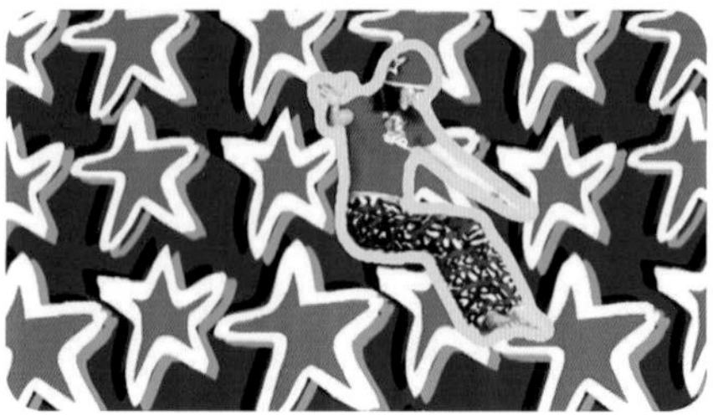

Stills from the
Stephen Sprouse
for Target TV
commercial

Joanne—our mother—did quite a lot of sewing when we were young. She would take us to L.S. Ayres in Indianapolis while she searched for fabric. She'd run her fingers through the fabric, look at colors, look at her patterns. Stephen would be just one step behind, mimicking her every move ... I remember at a very young age Stephen hand-sketching his own Spring and Fall fashion collections. He always had an uncompromising eye for detail. Our uncle used to draw automobiles on his arm when we spent the night. Stephen then began drawing on his own arm and later in life used his arm as a notepad.

Brad Sprouse, brother of the late Stephen Sprouse

KODAK 160VC

When Icons Met

Like any future-facing genius, Sprouse (pictured here, stepping into frame on his Target shoot) had his share of muses. One of them was Blondie frontwoman and New Wave fashion icon Deborah Harry, who combined glamour with a CBGB's edge. Sprouse came of age in the buzzing hive of late 70s downtown New York. In 1975, after he stopped working for the legendary brand Halston, he and Harry moved into a loft in the Bowery. She fed his cats, and he guided her style, merging her punk roots with his high-fashion background.

"I had a black trenchcoat, and Steve put it together with a pair of thigh-high boots and a little black dress and a beret, and I felt completely cool," said Harry in an interview with *W*. "That was one of my best-known looks. He also gave me a pair of Courrèges boots that I'd wear with fluorescent pink stretch pants. There was a real sense of play."

In 1979, Sprouse designed the dress Harry wore in Blondie's video for "Heart of Glass." He took a photo of TV scan lines and printed the image onto fabric, cleverly foreshadowing the mass-media-obsessed 80s just around the corner. Sprouse loved using production techniques far ahead of his time. "I remember the first color-Xerox machine in New York was on Sixth Avenue and 12th Street, and I would go and spend hours there," he told Harry, in a conversation for *Interview*. "Then I started getting into big stuff. It's all about blowups. I blew you up in the 70s."

Their friendship continued for years. In 1987, Sprouse launched his massive flagship store in SoHo, and Harry performed on a stage shaped as a large red "X."

But Harry—and Target—weren't Sprouse's only creative partnerships. Like Warhol, who worked with the other bright, boundary-pushing sparks of his day, Sprouse seemed to find electricity in collaborating. He splashed prints by Keith Haring across his 1988 Fall collection. He designed clothes for Duran Duran's 1989 tour, and their greatest hits album *Decade*, released the same year. He dressed Billy Idol for his comeback tour. Worlds and visions collided in unexpected ways. That's when magic happened.

If Warhol were alive today, he'd totally be doing stuff for Target.

Stephen Sprouse

Warhol, Bullseyes, and Design for All

We've always loved Andy Warhol's command of art and design, at once pop-infused, unconventional and produced in multiples. It's why in 2012, for the 50th anniversary of the first exhibition of Warhol's soup can silkscreens, we partnered with the artist's estate and Campbell's for a special collection—not on gallery walls but on Target shelves: elevating a kitchen staple into miniature, affordable works of art. We created 1.2 million cans in four brilliant, Warholian color combinations. Each one sold for 75 cents.

Warhol thought beauty should be available to everyone, an idea we've put into action through 20 years of our design collaborations. It's no surprise his first job was as a graphic designer for New York department stores. In the 50s, before he became a titan of art and culture, Warhol reimagined storefront windows for Bonwit Teller—a retailer that also helped launch the careers of Salvador Dali and Robert Rauschenberg.

While other storefront artists often didn't attach their names to their work, Warhol's bore his signature. He thought of advertising as a vehicle for celebrating and democratizing imagination, capable of spreading his work far and wide. He carried this mindset into the 60s, to the revolutionary Pop Art he helped pioneer.

Just as Warhol was drawn to the brightest lights of his era, from Marilyn Monroe to Edie Sedgwick, our collaborations begin with a love of boundary-pushing contemporary artists and designers. Our teams, from product design and engineering to marketing, work with them closely, dreaming together to expand their vision, to develop ideas they hadn't believed possible. Like Warhol, we are constantly inspired by the beauty in the everyday. And so we continue looking forward, designing new ways to share that joy with everyone.

Campbell's®
CONDENSED
PARIS INTERNATIONAL EXPOSITION
1900
TOMATO
SOUP
NET WT. 10 3/4 OZ. (305g)
Campbell's®
CONDENSED
PARIS INTERNATIONAL EXPOSITION
1900
TOMATO
SOUP
NET WT. 10 3/4 OZ. (305g)
Campbell's®
CONDENSED
PARIS INTERNATIONAL EXPOSITION
1900
TOMATO
SOUP
NET WT. 10 3/4 OZ. (305g)
Campbell's
CONDENSED
PARIS INTERNATIONAL EXPOSITION
1900
TOMATO
SOUP

Campbell's
CONDENSED
PARIS INTERNATIONAL EXPOSITION
1900
TOMATO
SOUP
NET WT. 10 3/4 OZ. (305g)
Campbell's
CONDENSED
PARIS INTERNATIONAL EXPOSITION
1900
TOMATO
SOUP
NET WT. 10 3/4 OZ. (305g)
Campbell's
CONDENSED
PARIS INTERNATIONAL EXPOSITION
1900
SOUP
NET WT. 10 3/4 OZ. (305g)
Campbell's
CONDENSED
PARIS INTERNATIONAL EXPOSITION
1900
TOMATO
SOUP
NET WT. 10 3/4 OZ. (305g)

In the Beginning, There Was a Toaster

Afterword by Molly Young

There's an old saying that goes something like this: "Fast, cheap, or good. Pick two." Meaning: we all want excellent things quickly and cheaply, but in reality we're lucky to nab two out of the three. The Target promise is a merry rejoinder to this seemingly iron law of life. "Expect More. Pay Less." Talk about a lofty standard to set. The functional translation of the tagline may as well be: "We defy the laws of consumer society. Welcome!"

The notion of providing treasured goods at an affordable price and with maximum convenience is, after all, something that looks nice when scribbled on a whiteboard but faces steep odds in reality. How does an enormous retailer offer an experience that is simultaneously affordable and premium? How can a product be special without being exclusive? How does a company refashion a consumer mindset that (often correctly) associates low price with low quality? Again: questions that are easy to lob around a conference room and tough to translate into reality—that is, the spin-resistant zone of shelves and supply chains and inventory.

And yet, the shopping public has never been more visually sophisticated. Each leap forward in the timeline of visual technology has brought aesthetic appreciation—formerly the playground of elites—to a wider audience. Paintings, printing, books, movies, television: as images have become cheaper and more abundant, ever-increasing ripples of humankind have developed visual literacy and with it, of course, personal taste. Thanks to the most recent of these interventions—the internet—there has never before been a moment in history when more people are more closely attuned to the nuances of the visual world. An 11-year-old girl in Tallahassee can analyze landscapes of the Florentine Renaissance without setting foot in Milan. She can wake up the next day and embark upon a digital tour of sixth-century Chinese silk production, pause for a morning snack, and then turn her attention toward protest posters of post-revolution Cuba. It's not unlikely that a preteen today has absorbed a greater volume and variety of visual input than her grandparents did in a lifetime. Design has never had a more discerning audience.

It has also never had a bigger platform. It's no surprise that the wilds of digital space, unlimited and teeming and handily accessible through devices that we can tuck into our pockets, has ignited a hunger for beautiful things. Seemingly infinite Pinterest boards and Instagram accounts testify to this appetite. Sating that hunger in the three-dimensional world, however, is much trickier. The production and distribution of tangible goods remains earthbound; the rules of physics apply. When it comes to connecting these far-off dots, however, it's fair to say that Target was an early adopter.

I turned 14 during a summer of the early aughts and, through some mystical parental covenant, was suddenly eligible to babysit local kids. This meant my feeble allowance was now supplemented by the crisp cash of a dozen parents desperate to escape their little

What sounds like a simple hypothesis was actually a radical reimagining of a consumer base.

screamers for an evening out or an adults-only beach day. There's nothing quite like the *intoxication* of being suddenly able to *buy things*, I discovered. My stash grew. As the season sloped into autumn, I knew that I'd spend my earnings on back-to-school clothes. After years of wearing whatever my parents agreed to spend money on—durable garments, inevitably sporting a loud pattern to "hide the stains"—I would be empowered to enter the classroom dressed exactly how I chose. My clothes would no longer be an extension of the two people who happened to conceive me. They would be an extension of my inner self, my aspirational self, my future self. Pure, undiminished Molly.

It was a blunt surprise to discover that two months of babysitting dough did not cover even one-tenth of the mod-inspired creamsicle-hued skirt that I'd dog-eared in *Vogue*. When I wasn't wiping ice cream from uncooperative toddler mouths, I'd spent humid afternoons combing through a stack of magazines, carefully building a fantasy blueprint of my wardrobe. My funds seemed as limitless as the opportunities for personal reinvention. When I finally summoned the courage to call a designer boutique about an item I loved (tantalizingly listed in the magazine as "Price upon request"), I was so startled by the response that I hung up the phone without saying thank you. In retrospect: well, duh. It wouldn't be in *Vogue* if a 14-year-old could afford it. It wasn't the first time I confronted a gap between what I desired and what I could buy, but it was the first moment that gap struck me as an uncrossable abyss.

If I'd been a little older and equipped with a driver's license, I might have discovered the chasm was less daunting than imagined. It was 2003, and the Isaac Mizrahi for Target collection had just made landfall; the store was a 30-minute drive from our house. In a parallel universe, I could have purchased a bubblegum corduroy blazer and a rainbow color-blocked shirt from the same designer who'd sent Linda Evangelista down the runway in a flaming orange jumpsuit, the one who'd starred in a movie about his status as a fashion divinity. I could have had enough cash left over to buy the matching beret.

Target, it turned out, had predicted my yearning for accessible beauty about four years earlier. In 1999, Michael Graves debuted his set of domestic products for the company, marking the beginning of a 13-year partnership. The line of some 150 items included a hand mixer, coffee maker, ice bucket, teakettle, and other everyday objects. For as low as $3.99, a shopper could break off a piece of considerable design cachet and take it home with her. "People ask me, 'Why are you doing this?'" Graves told *The New Yorker* on the occasion of his Target debut. "I tell them, 'If I design a library in Denver, that's for the masses, so why not this sort of stuff?'"

Why not, indeed. It's easy to overlook the radical novelty of the Graves-Target partnership now that a couple of decades have passed. We live in a world where the so-called "high-low mix" has achieved platinum status as an emblem of taste, and we've

Opposite:
Molly Young
photographed by
Tom Newton

The 1999 "Pop Art" toaster by Michael Graves for Target, photographed by Brooklyn Museum

Was it a stroke of brilliance or an act of blasphemy? Frank Lloyd Wright never designed a fondue pot. Mies van der Rohe never designed an ice cream scoop.

grown accustomed to diffusion lines from couturiers and farm-to-table fast food. But in 1999 there was still a notable incongruity in the fact that Graves, a globally-lauded architect and the winner of a National Medal of Arts, had designed a $39.99 toaster with chrome accents and a user-friendly side switch for "manual popping" that was effortlessly available in 851 Target stores across the US. Was it a stroke of brilliance or an act of blasphemy? Frank Lloyd Wright never designed a fondue pot. Mies van der Rohe never designed an ice cream scoop.

It was the beginning of a new theory in retail, one suggesting innovative design at a reasonable price was a compelling consumer proposition. That a normal person—say, someone without tomes of aesthetic philosophy or fashion history stacked on her night table—might prefer to buy a potato peeler or a melamine tray that was not only functional but also expressive of her sensibility; that she might like to own a product that could provide meaning and invoke affection with every use. What sounds like a simple hypothesis was actually a radical reimagining of a consumer base. It required that a mass-market company treat its audience not as shoppers but as clients: individuals to be pleased and catered to rather than snared and processed through a checkout line. (Incidentally, Target staff refer to their customers as "guests.")

Unsurprisingly, the mission to de-snobbify high design and fashion was risky—for both sides of the partnership. Artistic vision is an act of autonomy, which poses the practical question of how an organization might amplify a singular design perspective—that of Jean Paul Gaultier, Stephen Sprouse, or Alexander McQueen—without bending that vision, perhaps even inadvertently, to its own gravitational pull, potentially leaving the source material watery or unrecognizable. Is it possible to magnify an interesting idea without blowing it out of focus? This wasn't a new conundrum. The Bauhaus school of the early 20th century cherished the idea that great (and useful) design should be within the grasp of the average civilian, but nobody in 75 years had cracked the formula for turning that utopia into a reality.

Yet, somehow, it seemed to work here. And kept working. Target's partnerships ranged from the British fashion label Luella to the preppy princess of prints, Lilly Pulitzer, to Rodarte, a fashion label known for spending as long as 150 hours on a single dress, with the resulting garment perhaps more appropriate hung on a wall—like an artwork—than worn to a party. The

company quickly became defined by its multi-hued collaborations, opening to around-the-block lines. By its jolly lack of adherence to a hardboiled set of design constraints. By its eagerness to produce items that a person might encounter in a Target with the precise reaction of, "I did not expect to encounter this item in a Target." In an era when brand equity is everything and visual noise is deafening, it is not a stretch to call this philosophy of merchandising an audacious one.

The retail world has followed their lead. In recent years, a litany of others have recruited high-end designers to collaborate on affordable lines. Clothing brands began incorporating "curated" selections of outside products into their brick-and-mortar shops as a way of injecting surprise and borrowing prestige from smaller, cooler makers. The appetite for accessible design feels infinite; it would be shocking if it dissipated any time soon. With social media now a prime venue for people to production-design their own lives, access to inexpensive (but photogenic) accoutrements will only rise.

This doesn't mean collaborations between big brands and designers are easy to nail. I can't fathom an organizational challenge steeper than forging a bond of trust between an individual designer and a company that must interpret and execute at a mammoth scale.

I've never stepped foot inside Target's corporate headquarters or glimpsed the mystical process that results in such design synergies. I'd kill to know the secret sauce, the collaboration strategy, every detail of the workflow. I'm sure many others would, too. I do, however, own the fruits of a few collaborations. Target's head office might call me a "guest." There's the Anna Sui minidress with a crushed velvet periwinkle bow and tonal cuffs; I bought it at the tail end of my babysitting career. (It cost 3.5 hours of child-supervising.) There's the pair of glossy, earth-hued diagonally striped Missoni rain boots with this slogan printed on the shoebox: "Patterned after no one. Priced for everyone." And I've got an an ongoing eBay alert set up for "Michael Graves + Target + citrus juicer." I can't even explain how rare this thing is, or how beautiful. It's the color of a ripe satsuma, with a high gloss and a perfectly palm-sized handle. It is built for minimum hand exertion and maximum juice extraction. It is dishwasher safe. In years of vigilance, I've yet to find one on the secondary market. And when I do, my lemons won't know what hit them.

An elegant citrus juicer, by Michael Graves for Target

Index of Partnerships

Michael Graves, 1999-2013
Sonia Kashuk 1999—
Mossimo, 2000-2017
Philippe Starck, 2002
Stephen Sprouse, 2002
Andrea Immer-Robinson, 2002
Christopher Radko, 2002
David Kirk, 2002
Karim Rashid, 2002
Todd Oldham
  Home, 2002-2003
  Kid Made Modern, 2012—
  Hand Made Modern, 2015—
Liz Lange, 2002-2016
Cynthia Rowley and Ilene Rosenzweig, Swell, 2003-2006
Cynthia Rowley, Whim, 2008
Isaac Mizrahi, 2003-2009
Amy Coe, 2003-2007
Umberto Savone, 2004
Sean Conway, 2004-2010
Rachel Ashwell, Simple Shabby Chic 2004—
Fiorucci, 2005
Thomas O'Brien, 2005-2013
Deborah Adler, 2005-2015
Tord Boontje, 2006
Luella Bartley, 2006
Ayomi Yoshida, 2006
Paul and Joe, 2006
Tara Jarmon, 2006
Behnaz Sarafpour, 2006
Victoria Hagan, 2006-2010
Erin Fetherston, 2007
Proenza Schouler, 2007
Alice Temperley, 2007
Devi Kroell, 2007
Loeffler Randall, 2007
Keanan Duffty, 2007
Libertine, 2007
Rafé Totengco, 2007
Tracy Porter, 2007
Dominique Cohen, 2007
Isabelle de Borchgrave, 2007
Marcia Kilgore, 2007
Patrick Robinson, 2007
Holly Dunlap, 2007
DwellStudio, 2008
Jonathan Saunders, 2008
Terracycle, 2008
Anya Hindmarch, 2008
Jemma Kidd, 2008
Sigerson Morrison, 2008
Richard Chai, 2008
Monica Botkier, 2008
Dean Harris, 2008
Joy Gryson, 2008
Justin Giunta, 2008
Jovovich-Hawk, 2008
Rogan Gregory, 2008
Napoleon Perdis, 2008
Pixi, 2008—
Sami Hayek, 2008
Hayden Hartnett, 2008
Thakoon, 2008
Shaun White, 2008-2015
John Derian, 2008+2010
Anna Sui, 2009
Rodarte, 2009
Alexander McQueen, 2009
Orla Kiely, 2009
MIO, 2009
Tracy Feith, 2009
Paul Frank, 2009
Anna Sheffield, 2009
Carlos Falchi, 2009
Dror, 2009
Erickson Beamon, 2009
Felix Rey, 2009
Loomstate, 2009
Simone Legno, 2009
Miss Trish of Capri, 2009
Hollywood Intuition, 2009
Marcel Wanders, 2009
Jean Paul Gaultier, 2010
Liberty London, 2010
Stephen Burrows, 2010
Isabel and Ruben Toledo, 2010
Marcus Samuelsson, 2010
Poketo, 2010
Zac Posen, 2010
Eugenia Kim, 2010
Temple St. Clair, 2010
Trace Ayala and Justin Timberlake, William Rast, 2010
Cynthia Vincent, 2010
Tucker, 2010
Gianna Meliani, 2010

Mulberry, 2010
Dolce Vita, 2010
Simon Doonan, 2010
Giada De Laurentiis, 2010-2013
Missoni, 2011
Albertus Swanepoel, 2011
Appaman, 2011
Calypso St. Barth, 2011
Hamilton Wood Type & Printing
Museum, 2011
Josie Natori, 2011
Dana Kellin, 2011
Go Collective, 2011
Gwen Stefani, Harajuku Mini,
2011-2012
Jason Wu, 2012

Neiman Marcus, 2012
Joseph Altuzarra
Jason Wu
Proenza Schouler
Rodarte
Thom Browne
Band of Outsiders
Carolina Herrera
Derek Lam
Diane von Furstenberg
Marc Jacobs
Marchesa
Oscar de la Renta
Philip Crangi
rag & bone
Alice + Olivia
Judith Leiber
Tracy Reese
Lela Rose
Brian Atwood
Eddie Borgo
Prabal Gurung
Robert Rodriguez
Skaist-Taylor
Tory Burch

The Shops at Target, 2012
Cos Bar
Kirna Zabête
Odin
Patch NYC
Polkadog Bakery
Privet House
The Candy Store
The Curiosity Shoppe
The Webster

St. Tropez, 2012
Nate Berkus, 2012-2018
3.1 Phillip Lim, 2013
Prabal Gurung, 2013
Kate Young, 2013
FEED, 2013
Chris March, 2013+2014
Jeff Canham, 2014
Renee Kalfus-Annie Collection,
2014
Altuzarra, 2014
Peter Pilotto, 2014
Poppytalk, 2014
Wit & Delight, 2014
STORY, 2014
Oh Joy!, 2014-2017
TOMS, 2014
Eddie Borgo, 2015
Todd Snyder, 2015
Lilly Pulitzer, 2015
Adam Lippes, 2015
Dwell Magazine, 2016-2017
Marimekko, 2016
SoulCycle, 2016
Victoria Beckham, 2017
Accompany, 2017
Anna Kaiser, 2017
Print All Over Me, 2017
Chip and Joanna Gaines,
Hearth & Hand, 2017—
Hunter, 2018
Askov Finlayson, 2018
Museum of Ice Cream, 2018
Vital Voices, 2018
Leanne Ford, 2019
Vineyard Vines, 2019

Credits

© Alex Prager, p. 78-79, 80-81; © Andreas Sjodin / Trunk Archive, p. 205; © Anita Calero / Supervision, p. 178-179, 180; © Ann Ray, p. 284; Courtesy Art + Commerce, p. 220-221, 224-225; © Asko Tolonen / Designmuseum, Helsinki; © Autumn DeWilde, p. 322-323, 325, 326-327; © Barbara Anastacio, p. 106, 108; © Ben Pogue, p. 120-121; © Ben Weller / Trunk Archive, p. 136-137; © BFA, p. 246; © Brian Aris, p. 330; © Brian Edwards, p. 274; © Bryan Derballa, p. 77 (top); © Charles O. Cecil / Alamy Stock Photo, p. 18; © Charles Tracy, p. 316-317; © Christian McDonald / Trunk Archive, p. 275; © Craig McDean / Art + Commerce, p. 135, 250-251, 252; © Daniel Jackson / Art + Commerce, p. 272-273; © Daniel King, p. 215; © Darius Khondji, p. 146, 150; © Daymion Mardel / Art Department, p. 175; courtesy Deborah Adler, p. 50; © Denise Behrens, p. 248; © Dewey Nicks / Trunk Archive, p. 210; courtesy Design Guys, p. 22, 31, 32-33 ; © Djamilla Rosa Cochran, p. 241; © Dusan Reljin, p. 270; © Ellen von Unwerth / Trunk Archive, p. 266-267, 268, 271, 278-279; © Evan Savitt, p. 124-125; © Evan Sung, p. 141; courtesy Filip Engstrom, p. 102-103; © Getty Images, p. 6, 19, 29, 72, 73, 86, 87, 98, 99, 132, 140, 157, 165, 166, 169, 171, 191, 193, 209, 247, 269, 277, 285, 294, 295, 302, 303, 307, 310, 311, 319, 320, 331; © Graham Brown, p. 52; © Horst Diekgerdes / Trunk Archive, p. 142, 143; © Ilan Rubin / Trunk Archive, p. 289; © Jacob Sutton, p. 256-257, 258, 259, 260-261; © Jamie McGregor Smith, p. 134; © Jason Kibbler / Trunk Archive, p. 262-263; © Jessica Flores, p. 228; © JUCO, p. 36-37; © KT Auleta / Truck Archive, p. 286, 287; courtesy Lauren Bush Lauren, p. 45; © Laurie Rosenwald/www.rosenworld.com, p. 297; © Maira Kalman, p. 8; © Matthew Williamson / Art Department, p. 181; © Mei Tao, p. 44; © Michele Laurita, p. 184-185, 187; © Nathaniel Goldberg / Trunk Archive, p. 238-239; © Neil Rasmus / BFA, p. 246; © Nicki Sebastian, p. 183; © Nick Waplington, p. 200; © Pamela Hanson / Trunk Archive, p. 222; courtesy Paper magazine, p. 12-13; © Patrick McMullan, p. 277; © Paul Nelson, p. 214, 219; © Peter Lindbergh, p. 230-231, 232; © Rainer Hosch, p. 334-335, 338-339; © Richard Burbridge / Art + Commerce, p. 161; courtesy Sanji Senake, p. 156; © Sarah Silver / Trunk Archive, p. 240; © Sean Meszaros, p. 186; © Shutterstock, p. 318 ; © Silvia Razgova, p. 25; © Simon Burstall / Trunk Archive, p. 112; © Simon Cave, p. 233; courtesy Spring Studio, p. 147; © Stephen Allen, p. 158, 159; courtesy Steven Murashige, p. 60; © Susie Montagna, p. 148, 149; courtesy Tavi Gevinson, p. 324; © Terry Richardson / Art Partner, p. 244-245; © The Andy Warhol Foundation for the Visual Arts, Inc./Licensed by Artists Rights Society (ARS), New York (silkscreen) p. 30, 342-343; courtesy The Casting Studio, p. 90-91; © Tim Gutt, p. 212-213, 216-217, 218; © Tom Newton, p. 344; © Tom Schrimacher / Trunk Archive, p. 54-55, 58; courtesy TOMS Malaysia, p. 57; *Merimekko Logs, Helsinki, 1964* by © Tony Vaccaro / Tony Vaccaro Archives, p. 118; © Vincent Dilio, p. 288, 291; Insert poster: © Getty (left to right: Washington Memorial, Truman Capote, Fiorucci, Jacqueline Kennedy Onasis, Kennedy Family)

Acknowledgments

We would like to thank the thousands of people who have been involved in the last two decades of design partnerships—who have helped create and champion a vision of "Design for All." From designers to editors, photographers to influencers, creative agencies to team members, and guests to avid fans, we're grateful to every one of them for being part of our story.

First published in the
United States of America in 2019 by
Rizzoli International Publications, Inc.
300 Park Avenue South
New York, NY 10010

www.rizzoliusa.com

Publisher: Charles Miers
Associate Publisher: Anthony Petrillose
Editorial Coordination: Gisela Aguilar
Design Coordinator: Olivia Russin
Production Manager: Maria Pia Gramaglia
Managing Editor: Lynn Scrabis

**Built in partnership with
Chandelier Creative**

Printed in Italy

2019 2020 2021 2022 / 10 9 8 7 6 5 4 3 2 1
ISBN: 978-0-8478-6736-3
Library of Congress Control Number:
2019938315

Visit us online:
Facebook.com/RizzoliNewYork
Twitter: @Rizzoli_Books
Instagram.com/RizzoliBooks
Pinterest.com/RizzoliBooks
Youtube.com/user/RizzoliNY
Issuu.com/Rizzoli

“The Target collaborations have been a total game changer in terms of my personal style. Having the opportunity to own pieces I had once admired on celebrities—that would otherwise be out of reach for me—is incredible. I once camped out overnight to make sure I was first in line!”

Schevashea Carr (@curveebeauty)